Also by David Rosenberg

THE BOOK OF J
(with Harold Bloom)

A POET'S BIBLE

THE LOST BOOK OF PARADISE

*Anthologies Edited by
David Rosenberg*

CONGREGATION:
Contemporary Writers Read the Jewish Bible

TESTIMONY:
Contemporary Writers Make the Holocaust Personal

THE MOVIE THAT CHANGED
MY LIFE

COMMUNION:
Contemporary Writers Reveal the Bible in Their Lives

GENESIS:
As It Is Written

The

BOOK

of

DAVID

*A New Story of the Spiritual Warrior and Leader
Who Shaped Our Inner Consciousness*

DAVID ROSENBERG

Three Rivers Press
NEW YORK

Published by Three Rivers Press, a division of Crown Publishers, Inc., 201 East 50th Street, New York, New York 10022. Member of the Crown Publishing Group.

Originally published in hardcover by Harmony Books in 1997.

Random House, Inc. New York, Toronto, London, Sydney, Auckland

www.randomhouse.com

THREE RIVERS PRESS and colophon are trademarks of Crown Publishers, Inc.

Printed in the United States of America

Design by Lynne Amft

Library of Congress Cataloging-in-Publication Data
Rosenberg, David.
The book of David : a new story of the spiritual warrior and
leader who shaped our inner consciousness / by David Rosenberg.—
1st ed.
p.   cm.
1. David, King of Israel.   2. Bible. O.T. Samuel, 2nd, IX,
1-Kings, 1st, I, 5—Biography.   3. Bible. O.T. Samuel, 2nd, IX,
1-Kings, 1st, I, 5—Authorship.   4. Bible. O.T. Psalms—
Authorship. I. Bible. O.T. Samuel, 2nd, IX, 1-Kings, 1st, I,
5. II. Bible. O.T. Psalms.   III. Title.
BS580.D3R625   1997
222'.4092—dc21
[B]   97-14061
CIP

ISBN 0-609-80225-9

10 9 8 7 6 5 4 3 2 1

First Paperback Edition

To the memory of
Yitzhak Rabin, leader
and David Avidan, poet
too soon gone

$\mathcal{A}cknowledgments$

Caring words from those close to me helped sustain this work. When I thought it was nearly finished, it came before the enlightened attention of my editor, Shaye Areheart, and her assistant editor, Dina Siciliano, who helped me to transform it into a braver book. Lew Grimes, my literary agent, first found this book its fortunate home. The ancient Hebraic culture we are now beginning to restore would have needed similarly creative people to nurture it. Peers in other fields and cultures would have been as necessary then as they are today, and I was inspired by encouraging words from Laurie Anderson, Arthur Miller, David Mamet, Greil Marcus, Jeanette Winterson, Andrew Motion, Moshe Idel, Ivan Schwebel, Harold Schimmel, Michal Govrin, Claire Bloom, Fritz Weaver, Mimi Gross, Miro Davis, David Smith, Walter Brown, David Lee, and Peter Raven. It comes down to inspiration. I was inspired by Shifra and Milton, Wanda and Bertram, my witty parents, and Rhonda, my wife, coauthor of every word. In addition, Rhonda Rosenberg's luminous critique, which appears in this book's appendix, preserved my spirit.

—David Rosenberg

Contents

The BOOK of DAVID

Prologue: Authoring a Life

How men and women imagine their lives today begins with the mature David. His story and his own writing thrive on intimacy and breaking barriers. He is a fertile resource in a time when boundaries of gender, nature, and belief are in question.

David embodied an inner consciousness newly in tune with an outer world of human and social creations. Writing in the new Hebraic alphabet, his psalms showed how to communicate from the inside, while his actions as a leader inspired candor in his court historian. He revealed how human culture is a reflection of an original intimacy with the world, and how that first bond remains our spiritual foundation.

The older type of hero, represented by King Saul, when faced with uncertainty just said no (and lost his mind). But change is more complicated, and David is aware, inventive and vulnerable when facing it. His life story suggests that when the outer doesn't jibe with the inner perception, the resulting ambiguity requires a new focus. Sometimes we might want to laugh and cry at the same time, for instance, and when we can accept the split feelings as a new feeling, we enter the realm of David.

The mystery of God inherent in the world religions is reflected on the human scale in the complications of intimacy. The difficulty was often transcended in faith and in past codes of chivalry—especially in the eyes of men. Yet for David himself, the complexities of intimacy were worked out in the world of men and women, and in writing. David's psalms are the original "God talk," revealing a love of intimacy in all its aspects.

I thought of how my own confusion about intimacy once walled me off from the irony of my origins and early memories. The way adults seemed to withdraw from each other's anxieties showed me how to withdraw into sports and then books, and there I found (irony of ironies!) that intimacy was at the core of all human portrayals. At a certain point I even wondered if I would be able to match in real life the intimacy of translating a dead poet. David, however, shows us how we are all more than what we think we are. He faced and unified ambiguities in himself; he reconciled inner with outer worlds; and he inspired other writers to translate his actions into words.

It wasn't so long ago that the differences between cultures were stressed. Now, the similarities can be even more enlightening. Instead of a striking difference between body and mind, today the complexity of their alliance is more to the point. To be able to hold in mind—side by side—laughter and tears, objectivity and fear, affords a fullness. And this quality, so original in David, allows us to be fulfilled when the ambiguous loyalties in others and in ourselves threaten to tear us in two.

Of course, the split between flesh and spirit is represented in all cultures. Aboriginal masks transform the body into an ambiguous duality: part human, part other. Beyond masks, our own transcendent art may be traced to David. In place of direct messages from the divine, David's court writers retold the encounters of patriarchs and prophets in narrative. Nathan the prophet brings a divine message to David, reminding him of his adultery with Bathsheba, but it is couched in a story that David is able to internalize. And from the day that the story of Jacob's wrestling with an angel was given an ambiguous quality by a writer at David's son Solomon's court, culture and religion has remained irretrievably mixed. To untangle the confusions, I was led back to origins, to David.

The author of David's mature life stretches for a new kind of complexity to live by. The old legends show David overcoming obstacles; for example, he fought against grandiosity, embodied in the caricature of Goliath. But a new story was needed then, and it is needed today as well. When the boundaries between history and imagination are broken, a story about the battle for consciousness becomes primary. By shaping the way an individual life can be written, David shows us how to rewrite our own. The new story of David's life puts the author back into the story. David's spirit demands we hold in mind both story and author—both our present and our origin.

With David it is possible to laugh and cry together, and not simply one or the other. The crying part of ourselves—the observer—is aware of the loss that the laughing, unknowing part is not. Faith becomes mortal: it can be lost. We cannot so simply laugh or cry anymore, for every new surprise revelation reminds us we have lost faith in an old convention. David transforms our losses into an intimacy in the world, and into an intimacy with poetry. And when we read David's subtlest biographer, we find that even when David is surrounded by highly entertaining characters, the drama centers on his personality. We become more intimate with his complexity while the others reflect facets of his character.

There are no bones to be found for historical characters of the Bible, but the bones of the writers are still before our eyes, embedded in their words. And there is a time for the bones to be breathed upon as well—to give them a reimagined life. After David, we cannot forget human authors anymore. To reclaim him today is to face again our most basic, creative origins. Many new trends in spiritual and self-help writings emphasize ways to "author" our lives. When we go back to our first authors, however, the questions we most need to ask are about inspiration. Where does it come from and how is it represented? David provides the richest answers. He inspires us to transform inner losses into creative acts.

INTRODUCTION

The New Story of David

The story of David must change now, irrevocably. There's been too much written about the creation of characters in the Bible, including the character of God. It is too late to continue repressing the knowledge that artful human beings with noted names wrote these provocative tales, often transforming oral material. Writers in ancient times were as sophisticated as those today, wearing the masks of selfhood and sometimes pretending to take them off, while delighting the audience of their day. Why has tradition suppressed their names and pretended instead that the writing was primitive and anonymous?

Who created David? The new answer: It was his author, a great Hebraic writer at the Solomonic court whom scholars call the Court Historian, or S, since his life of David is embedded in the Bible's books of Samuel. To face this author is to change everything. The simple vignettes and legends of David and Goliath, or David and Bathsheba, or David and Jonathan—scenes adaptable to musical comedy—will no longer do. The true life of David has become the story of the man who portrayed God in his own image: a creator stepping into the background of his tale.

Here is how the history of David must now be told. Long ago in our prehistory, Homo sapiens lived in the land that became Israel, cultivating trees and their fruits, making art and poetry, and eventually domesticating animals and words alike. The stories of our cultural life were inscribed on the skins of our animals in those days.

These indigenous Homo sapiens, exactly like us in their genes, became known as Hebrews, or wanderers, when they themselves were pushed to the margins by waves of foreigners from expanding empires. Similar to the experience of Native Americans, the Hebrew stories of ties to the land were repressed, and in their place came the new myths of a people whose origins lay in the civilizations of Egypt and Mesopotamia. Characters like Moses and Abraham effectively blocked the collective memory of roots in the land. It took centuries—just as it has for indigenous Americans—before the Hebrews were assimilated into the newer culture. But even then, many remained a people apart.

The new civilization evolved to produce a kingdom and a court of great writers, established three thousand years ago by King David in Jerusalem. Many years after David's death, and after his son Solomon's death, two professional writers at the Solomonic court created a new Hebraic renaissance. They recast old tales and poetry in the new Hebraic language. The great writer S, who was first a protégé and later a companion of J, was the son of an indigenous mother. He retold the story of David while conscious of the true history of the Hebrews in the land.

David's dependence on "outcasts," with whom he lived for years while hiding from Saul, the king who wanted to kill him, discloses his indigenous ties. From these people David learned the arts of poetry and leadership. His mother was also an indigenous woman, and she taught him the shaman songs that he would later transform into Hebraic psalms.

David was our first renaissance man: a poet and thinker, a warrior and peacemaker, a leader and innovator. How could one man be all these things? Character is the answer, according to S. Only a great writer could give David a strong yet believable character, a man of independent mind like his own. Many years later, tradition pushed the memory of David's author to the margins, and finally it became lost, along with the memory of a Hebraic renaissance. In place of roots in the land, the new tradition elaborated the conquering of the land, leading to the establishment of a conventional kingdom. But as the leader of his people, David was far from conventional. The time has come to confront the legends with a mature understanding of our origins. The story that was repressed can now be restored.

The new story of David changes us, turns us inside out, from a culture founded upon an ancient religion to one founded upon creativity, knowledge of intimacy, and self-knowledge. Instead of a tribal past, we have a cultural renaissance at our origin, restoring what had already been repressed and lost.

David has a mother, an indigenous woman with a natural history in the land. David has an author, a man whose own mother, an indigenous princess wed to King Solomon, sang him lullabies that he, too, would transform into our great poems, the psalms. S added a shield to David's character: an interior life, strengthening a character more complex and creative than otherwise imaginable.

David's author had a companion, J, who nurtured S in her image. And finally, the Book of David had a culture, a renaissance that can be reimagined. As it is restored to us, we gain a new depth of creative freedom. The libraries of the Davidic renaissance are lost, but we can sense the individual writer represented by his art: his or her distance from and irony toward the myths of their day and toward convention (only lesser writers identify fully with the conventional).

J and S and the hundreds of Hebraic writers and translators of their time were great *readers* first, confirmed by evidence of the library and archives at David's palace—these grand receptacles of a people's cultural and religious heritage were created before even a stone was laid for the Temple. The skins, scrolls, and tablets were read in silence by individuals who were writers themselves, and who could read several scripts, including many languages in cuneiform. They knew the work of other cultures and of their own past. The events they wrote about were already distant, a time of great poignance that had been lost and needed to be reimagined. Until now, we ourselves had lost the power to imagine this great culture of writers such as J and her protégé, S.

The evidence that J was a woman is first presented in a book Harold Bloom and I coauthored in 1990, called *The Book of J.* In it we explore, among other things, why J's style and vision is opposed to those of the other biblical writers. The females in her narrative, which runs from Adam and Eve to the death of Moses, often have more character than the males—while Joseph, whose charismatic life resembles that of David, is a moving exception. J's point of view is ironically nuanced toward the other males, yet, predictably, many experts are upset that one of our greatest writers was probably a woman.

One reason, perhaps, lies in facing the fact that the great writers of the Bible did not use biblical Hebrew; instead, they wrote in a more poetic, archaic Hebrew whose idiom is largely unknown to scholars. It takes a writer's imagination to probe the sensibility of those original authors. The writing of their language had just evolved from cuneiform and was in its renaissance at the Solomonic court: It was a time comparable to the Elizabethan. It is also no accident that writers today prefer the Elizabethan King James translation, since it is the only writerly translation we have.

How we read David can change our lives. His character is a map of spirit symbolized by interlocking triangles, David's star, which is also known as his shield. S gave David a shield to hold—a protective cover of character—to preserve him from the impersonal rage of war and from the vicissitudes of time. David's spirit was imbued with character that was irrepressible, and character becomes spirit and poetry in the transforming imagination of the author, S. Meanwhile, the king we know from legends in the Bible, the king who rules by conquering the land is a censored image of David handed down by tradition. The actual king in S's Book of David rules by creative inspiration. The prominence bestowed on his sensibility replaces conquest with culture, assimilating and restoring the arts of the land.

The evidence of David's rich creative life, of his guiding spirit and character, is best understood by imaginative writers. It isn't difficult to imagine the intimacy of the two great writers J and S because the early Bible itself is a love affair with writing, matured from the older oral forms. From a love affair of writing to a love affair of writers is a natural progression. Even more essential to the truth: The love affair between the Creator and David is so colored with human feeling that it is best represented by human creators.

I have asked myself again and again why tradition resists the human culture that produced the Bible. This reaction is visible today among the experts who attempt to erase or reduce authorship, returning it to the dank skeleton of structure. This repression has its price, and it diminishes the inspiration that gave voice to the writing.

Writers today, even though our modern culture keeps them at arm's length, can help us face facts: God can be an enigmatic character in the great stories, just like the gods in ancient Greek literature. But S went further, and we are richer for the knowledge that his character David, by interiorizing God, planted individual inspiration at our origin. The historical David's acts of writing, as rewritten by S, unified exterior and interior thought and feeling, and allowed a complexity of character that moved God into the background.

By showing inspiration to be an inner thing available to all individuals, David's repressed past became transformed. His interior life gave us the confessional psalms and the dynamic story of his life, because David's past was full of natural experience. Yet he remained God's beloved in the hands of our first writers, and we might be tempted to say that David was godlike. When we refer to the mastery of S, however, we are acknowledging the author's own creativity, and not his portrayal of David's power.

The final question becomes: Who are we, as David's descendants?

To be his readers today, we must be our own restorers of the truth. Perhaps it threatens the beliefs of some to face reality so directly, but I believe our spirit is transformed, in the process, into a source of creative inspiration, just as it was for David. He freed us from the pedants of his day by embodying an independent mind. By holding on to our independence, and restoring a heritage of great authors, we reveal who we are today as Davidic—and clear-eyed—readers.

> The sense of being immersed in a sentient world is preserved in the oral stories and songs of indigenous peoples—in the belief that sensible phenomena are all alive and aware, in the assumption that all things have the capacity of speech. Language, for oral peoples, is not a human invention but a gift of the land itself.
> —David Abram, *The Spell of the Sensuous: Perception and Language in a More-Than-Human World* (1996)

David the king might have spoken words like these about his indigenous ancestors. The words he composed for the earliest psalms transform oral knowledge into an interior world that speaks to the outer one in the form of the Creator. Immersed in his own self-awareness, David imagines the outer world created in a form of self-awareness also. David's confessional psalms thereby became a gift back to the land.

Is the early Hebrew Bible a rough and primitive work redeemed by the presence of God, as conventional critics still claim? Remove God, and what's left? Here's what: As we put aside the blinkers, we see that the Bible appears rough in places on purpose, in a conscious strategy by writers who shine a searching light of irony into the past. God and the author of David's mature life, S, merged into the background together. The creator of the story, in other words, is both omnipresent and hidden. By restoring the process of its artistic creation, we begin to heal our loss of belief in the quality of inspiration. So the book I have written, translated, and restored is a book about the inner world and writing as well as about our worldly origins.

To prepare for this restoration, I had to change my own life as well. After years of study in New York and Jerusalem, I moved to an area near the Florida Everglades, where I could experience an overwhelming ecosystem and its restoration by poet-scientists at the frontiers of our culture. How do we begin to repair an endangered ecosystem when we don't have enough evidence of what it was originally like? In the same way, we have no bones that identify J and S. Instead, what is required is a new openness and imagination for reading the past. Scholars and writers alike, who live out their lives in academic conclaves, are losing their instinct for inspiration. To regain it, we need to go back to the sources with fresh eyes and an open heart.

Chronology

B.C.E.	
32,410–30,340	World's oldest known great art discovered in the Chauvet cave of southern France, 1994
10,000–3500	Spread of agricultural communities throughout the Near East
3500	Invention of cylinder seals in southern Mesopotamia, used for sealing clay tablets written in cuneiform script
2400	Early cuneiform (syllabic) tablets and scrolls in Sumerian libraries
1700–1600	Descent of Hebrew tribes into Egypt
1650	Hittite libraries in the Middle East, including cuneiform texts and translations of Akkadian and other languages
1450	Cuneiform texts translated into alphabets: Phoenician and prototype of archaic Hebrew
1280	Exodus of Hebrews from Egypt
1250–1200	Conquest of Canaan
1200	Mycenaean Greek and Phoenician texts in "sea people" (Philistine) libraries in Middle East
1150–1000	First period of Hebraic books, including *The Book of the Wars of Yahweh*, *The Book of Paradise*, and *The Book of the History of Adam*
1020–1000	Samuel and Saul
1000–961	United Monarchy of David
961–922	Empire of Solomon
950–900	The Book of J
927	Death of Solomon; division of the kingdom

927–915	Reign of Rehoboam in Judah
917–900	The Book of David
850–800	First (E) revision of J
722–721	Fall of the Northern Kingdom of Israel
650–600	Deuteronomy
587–538	Fall of Jerusalem and Judah; the Babylonian Exile
550–500	The P text; another return from exile begins
400	The redactor of JEPD
380	The redactor of the Book of Samuel
100	Editing of Hebrew Bible completed

I

The

AUTHOR

at the

ORIGIN

of the

BIBLE

1

The Author S

What if we did not know that *Hamlet* was written in London during the Elizabethan renaissance. Imagine that a thousand years from now it is believed that *Hamlet* was an anonymous religious text written in South Africa in the nineteenth century by a Boer saint. Would that not make a difference in the way it is read? Or take the *Odyssey*: Imagine that we believe it was written in North Africa in the Carthaginian language and translated into Greek. Wouldn't we read the text differently, noting the Greek spin on its original meaning? Why is it we know more about the authors of these great works than we do about the the author of King David's brilliantly written life?

Today we are just beginning to learn more about the lost culture that wrote the foundation of the Bible. It was a renaissance in its time, when the great courts of David and Solomon assembled archives and libraries of archaic cuneiform writing, translating these works and others into the new Hebrew language and alphabet. Hebrew was as fresh and vibrant then as Elizabethan English was in Shakespeare's time.

Following a breakthrough in multicultural studies, we are also just discovering that many overlooked cultures are no less resourceful than our own. Some, like that of the ancient Hebrews, were considered important only for a single aspect such as religion, while the rest was rejected. There were many great writers of independent mind and sophistication, however, during the Hebraic renaissance that began in David's time. We need to reimagine the context of their lives, including their own recent past. We want to know who these authors might have been, how they thought, and what kinds of lives they lived. We deserve to reclaim their entire culture.

In Jerusalem, nearly three thousand years ago, a forgotten author designated as S—working as a writer, translator, and companion of the author of Genesis, J— composed a work that has determined the cultural consciousness of Western civilization: a life of David. We possess a coherent portion of that work, embedded within what we call 2 Samuel, of the Bible's books of Samuel.

Although we cannot know the exact circumstances under which the work was written, we can observe the resemblances and differences in style, in content and in art, between S's narrative and J's, as well as between S and other biblical authors. Recently, some scholars have become obsessed with separating S from other authors in Samuel, denoting them S1, S2, S3, and so on. But this must be considered an academic exercise, since there is only one author whose artistry has been claimed by generations of scholars: the "Court Historian," or S. Why has the work of S never been detached from its surroundings and presented on its own terms? I first answered this question when I translated the *Book of J*: The scholarly taboo still exists against imagining the original writers as sexual human beings. And if there is a great novel, the Book of David, embedded in the Bible, why has it not been retranslated? Although many commentators refer to its literary quality in novelistic terms, the primary value attributed to S's work is historical. It would be as if Tolstoy's *War and Peace* had never been read as a novel but only as a documentary history of the Napoleonic wars and the lives of officials.

S's life of David is not a didactic work but a great work of art, and another reason it has not been appreciated is that religion finds it hard to acknowledge the Hebraic culture that produced the great writers of the Bible. Yet the courtier S at King Solomon's son's court was not more unusual a writer than those of a later renaissance in Elizabethan England—Sidney or Raleigh, Wyatt or Ben Jonson—who were also courtiers or near-courtiers writing for a small, elite audience of peers, and who rarely bothered with publication.

Like his elder, J (the term stands for Jahwist or Yahwist, after her designation for God, Yahweh, or Jehovah), S probably lived at the court of Solomon's son and successor, King Rehoboam of Judah. Rehoboam allowed his father's kingdom to fall apart in the 920s and 930s B.C. It has been shown likely that J was a woman, and even as I believe that S was a man, the evidence suggests that he was an intimate companion of J's. My colleague, Harold Bloom, has written about Genesis: "David is what, in J's judgment, Abram, Jacob, Tamar, and the others strive toward becoming." And as S's mentor and companion, J has bestowed her image of David upon S, who makes of him Yahweh's beloved.

What kind of career would S have had, given his talents? Most likely he would have been of Solomon's family, one of perhaps hundreds of princes, though not necessarily a son. Imagine that his mother, one of the vast number of foreign wives Solomon took for political reasons among others, would have been an aboriginal princess. This child was a prodigy and trained at court in languages.

All court writers would also have been translators, as the work of absorbing the older tradition and other cultures into the new alphabet and changing language required knowledge of cuneiform, perhaps even pictogram. As a prodigy, S would have won the notice of J, the older woman who was writing the fresh cultural history that began with the life of Adam and ended with the death of Moses. J was a Solomonic princess whose fame had elevated her authority above the need to teach at court, yet she might have cherished the role of tutor to S, being childless herself. Thus J might have become S's surrogate mother.

The image of Yahweh in S's court history is an image of J herself, a powerful presence largely in the background, great enough to forgive David his flaws with a constant belovedness, a "lovingkindness"—in

Hebrew, the word *chesed*, which weds love to ethics. David was beloved, loved as no man before him—by Yahweh.

J's mandate had been to create a unifying culture for Judah, so that Solomon's many foreign wives and their cultures could be assimilated. Lovingkindness was a Davidic theme she shared with S as she delegated to him the role of writing the court history of David. Lovingkindness, or covenantal ethics, was accompanied by a yearning for the land. These themes were of high indigenous significance, long before the Bible's Deuteronomist gave to *chesed* its pious meanings.

In a nonpareil of biography, history, and poetic fiction, S, the biblical author of the court history in 2 Samuel, forges a new genre as he writes the biography of monotheism. For the first time, a human being is portrayed in all his dimensions, inside and out, as made in the image of God. It is King David—and moreover, his mother is a mystery, named nowhere in the Bible. Yet there is a mothering presence in the book S wrote during his lifetime at the Solomonic court of Rehoboam—and it is Yahweh, the one God, creator and sustainer of human life. Throughout his biography of David, S's Yahweh stands in the background, rushing forward at crucial moments to encourage his beloved one, or to discipline him for his mistakes. Unlike the sometimes stern father God in J's Pentateuch, who forbids his Moses to enter the Promised Land, the God in S's book is always there for his beloved king, David, as we expect a mother to be.

Now, who was David's human mother and why is she erased from text and tradition? I believe that S had no need to name her in his portrait of David because she was known at the time and Yahweh stands for her loving character as well as her ancient roots in the land and in religion. She was one of Jesse's many wives, the last and youngest, with whom he had his last child, David. She was a Canaanite princess, but not a significant one, not a daughter of a major tribe. She was, rather, an aboriginal princess, daughter of one of the "outcast" indigenous people camped outside the city of Bethlehem. Jesse no doubt hired men in her family to work in his field and women of her family to work in his house. Perhaps she had actually been a handmaid in his house when he fell in love with her—for it was surely a great love, and David was the most beloved of sons.

And what of the mother of S, the Hebrew author? Since she was also an aboriginal Canaanite princess, S was on familiar ground in his portrayal of David. J, when she commissioned S after a long tutoring, knew from the start that he would be uniquely qualified by his background. And he was as a son to her. He was close to being the beloved who never lost his sense of loyalty—who retained a sense of shared lovingkindness between his mentor and himself. It could not be otherwise; the depth of playful intimacy shared by the two texts these great authors produced, foundation to the Pentateuch and the books of Samuel, would have required a friendship difficult to maintain were there not a sexual bond, however sublimated.

If David was at least part aboriginal, and if he transmitted to the Jews his mother's culture, then it was of a people exiled in their own land, the indigenous people of Canaan. As Moses stands for the new religion, David represents the new Hebraic culture, its written tradition, and its transforming powers. Most of all, David represents roots in the land. His promised land lies in a memory of having lost and regained it. As we see in his biblical biography and in the psalms that S composed in his name, David is a master of transforming the sorrow of loss into celebration. The Bible's version of the conquest of the land of Israel (originally Canaan) coming on a promise from God is essentially a mask over a regaining of land lost. David's ancestors cannot be imagined coming from anywhere else; his character is indigenous to Israel.

Later tradition affirms my hypothesis in one surprising allusion to David's mother. In a volume of *Yalkut*, in the Midrash, A. S. Rappoport translates, "In spite of his great piety, Jesse was not quite free from temptation. He possessed a beautiful slave upon whom he had cast his eyes, and one day he made up his mind to set the slave free and marry her. The fruit of this union was David. And Jesse esteemed David lightly.

The supposed son of a slave was not educated with the other sons. David was sent to tend the sheep." So we can understand how the mystery of David's birth may have long been associated with an aboriginal mother, as the term *slave* unfortunately conjures.

Yet there is no reason to believe that David was not a beloved son of his real mother, just as he was of Yahweh. It is only much later, after the first flowering of Hebraic culture, that the repression of aboriginal roots becomes an obsession. Considered carefully, the connotation of a slave is here subconsciously allied with a wish to forget the exile and enslavement—both in Egypt and within ancestral Canaan.

In his last work Sigmund Freud writes, "The history of King David and his time is most probably the work of one of his contemporaries." On a page earlier in that book, *Moses and Monotheism*, J is described as "the author in which the most modern research workers think they can recognize Ebjatar, a contemporary of King David." Freud goes no further in imagining the relationship of J and S, but he had imagined their greatness as authors and their common culture at a time, more than fifty years ago, when most biblical scholars were afraid to even mention a biblical writer. In the intervening years, repression has actually deepened, so that Freud's late work remains far advanced of the field.

Freud hypothesizes the Egyptian influence at the Davidic court, and in an earlier book of mine, *The Lost Book of Paradise*, I followed his hint in imagining the Hebraic scholar Devorah Bat-David, who was born into the Jewish exilic community of Elephantine, Egypt. Devorah was integral to a court culture made up of hundreds of translators and writers—especially translators, since the dominant activity in building the Hebraic culture was translating the cuneiform classics (including Mosaic writings and oral tradition) into the new Hebrew alphabet. I did not speculate about its origins, but I find now, as I reread Freud, that he conjectures "that early Israelites, the scribes of Moses, had a hand in the invention of the first alphabet." I prefer to concentrate on the later cosmopolitan culture at the Davidic and Solomonic courts, but the fact remains that remote times hold a great attraction, as Freud pointed out in *Moses and Monotheism:* "As often as mankind is dissatisfied with its present—and that happens often enough—it harks back to the past." By the time of Rehoboam's court, when I believe J and S were in their prime, the elite who could read and write were no doubt distraught about their present, yearning for a golden past that David already represented, having succeeded Moses.

It was precisely this longing that both J and S could play upon, and it allowed S the freedom to embody in David a combination of the happiest and most tragic of Hebraic characters, a type of indigenous ideal that S might have studied in his own aboriginal background. So that by the time of the Bible's first great writers, J and S, the golden age was already lost—and in its wake came a glorious renaissance of Hebraic culture and writing.

Is it crucial how accurate the "history writing" was? According to a distinguished biblical scholar, Moshe Weinfeld, in *The Promise of the Land* (1993), a close reading reveals that "enclaves of the Canaanite peoples remained and Canaanites continued to live in various cities in the land of Israel, such as Jerusalem, Gezer, Beth-shean, Megiddo, Acco, and other cities on the coast and in the valleys." Yet the Bible pretends not to distinguish between foreign and aboriginal Canaanites, the "outcasts" whom David alone embraces. May we wonder why? Freud makes it clear that the desire to repress humble origins—and embellish tales of heroic patriarchs—is natural, and few cultures do not look down upon aboriginal peoples as "primitive." Yet more than in any other parts of the Bible, we find in both J and S the traces of true fondness for "outcast peoples."

Would S have been distressed by the sufferings inflicted upon the Canaanites under David and Solomon? Probably not, since the aboriginal peoples by this time would have been largely assimilated among the Jews, and S's own mother, among the last aboriginal princesses, might have been wed by Solomon for sentimental reasons as much as political ones. The Bible tells us of Solomon's hundreds of wives. Perhaps Solomon wanted to honor—but not have to remember in specific detail—his father David's embrace of these outcasts, which might include the exotic designations S presents in his narrative, among them "Cherethites," and "Pelethites," and "Archites," and "Gittites." Any of them might be aboriginal peoples.

By Rehoboam's time it must have been mostly forgotten that the Hebrews were once an aboriginal people. Traces of it would have been erased for the "primitive" associations just as the writers were to be erased in later centuries. S himself would have felt at least as authentic a Jew as his counterparts from the Egyptian slavery—perhaps the way, today, the Yemenite and Ethiopian Jews in Israel command authenticity. His work was to imprint the greatness of his aboriginal culture on the culture of the new Jewish nation. To S, Israel *was* an Indian nation transformed through the symbolic David into a cosmopolitan culture at home in the land once again, as in ancient days.

No doubt the religion would have been transformed as well, but this would have seemed secondary at the time. There was no need to mock the idols of other religions when the Hebrews continued to acknowledge them through several succeeding centuries. Solomon's embrace of foreign and Canaanite religions through his wives would not have shocked anyone then, for the Hebrew culture remained dominant and that was what counted. Hebrew was for a time a new lingua franca, and all foreign cultures were being translated into the Hebrew alphabet by Jewish translator-poets. Like S, these poets were schooled at court to adapt the cuneiform texts of foreign libraries into ones with a Jewish perspective.

When we think about it, it seems strange it was not thought about before: The basis of the Bible, the Holy Land, is an indigenous people's concept. Yet the Bible tells us that the Hebrews were a wandering people, the patriarchs coming from a civilization to the east, Mesopotamia, growing into a seminomadic tribe of shepherds. This story derives from the founding myths of other cultures of the period. It is a moving story, but it is still a cover story. No proud civilization wished to describe their origins as indigenous or native or primitive. The Hebraic culture of David's time must have felt itself becoming as sophisticated as parts of Greece or Egypt, and it wished to screen out the memory of a primitive background in the land. Citizens did not want to see themselves as if they came from the Indians or native people of Canaan, yet it seems likely that these early Jews were tied to the land in deeper ways than any other culture was. They became the nation of David and Solomon after turning their history into stories and later into the great poetic narratives retold by the professional class of writers at court, who rewrote with inspired imagination.

Which version of their storied history did the biblical writers of this time actually believe? Consider: Which version of our American story of the conquest of the West do you believe? If a writer today tells the story as a war of conquest against the respected powers of the Indians, it will certainly be with irony. There was little respect for Indians, and we know it. We know from other sources that the catastrophic losses of the native cultures were the result of disrespect, indifference, and even loathing. In the same way, the story of the conquest of Canaan by the twelve tribes must have been read with irony by the educated class of readers surrounding the king's court in David and Solomon's day. Instead, they most likely knew that their tribal roots were in the land and that they had long ago been uprooted by conquering invaders from settled civilizations.

It must be stressed that the context today of claims to the land is rendered an irrelevant issue. Jews and Arabs have equal claims to aboriginal roots; the fundamental difference is that aboriginal culture determined the Jewish one to a far greater degree than it did any other. We can see this in many aspects of the Bible, and impressively preserved in the work of S. More than in most civilizations, aboriginal influence seems profoundly embedded in the original Hebraic culture that produced the refined writers of the Bible.

2

The Hebrews: An Indigenous History

Let us consider who the aboriginals in Canaan truly were. As described in biblical history, they were not an indigenous people but, rather, former colonists who brought with them the cultures of Mesopotamia, Egypt, Crete, and other agricultural nations. The Bible describes them as city-builders and idol worshipers, with their "abominations" revolving around gods who controlled the destiny of the annual crops.

The original Canaanites, the indigenous people of what later became Israel, had to be quite different from these and from the Hittites and Philistines, or the "Edomites and Perrizites," with whom King Saul and King David battled in the tenth century B.C. The indigenous people would not have been farmers but shepherds and subsistence farmers, more gatherers than hunters. Instead of agriculture, their true talent was horticulture: They pioneered the cultivation of trees—fruit trees especially, such as dates and figs. Their settled villages were dedicated to the tending of groves of trees, including olives, and also nuts and grapes.

In the Bible, only the Jews themselves most resembled these natives. They stand out from all other cultures just as the indigenous people did. And in a fundamental way, the Jewish culture that produced the great stories of the Bible resembles these native Canaanites as does none other. Both Jews and indigenous peoples worshiped the land and built their cultures on a relationship to it that went far deeper than their civilized colonizers. This relationship to the land has recently been explored in depth by Moshe Weinfeld, who teaches at the Hebrew University in Jerusalem. Weinfeld determines that the biblical traditions of covenant and divine promise, of sin and redemption, are tied to a deep identity with the land itself and a fear of losing it, of being assimilated by the surrounding civilizations. Here is precisely the identity and dread of exile that one would expect of an indigenous people.

Could the Hebrew tribes, then, have sprung from the remnants of dispossesed indigenous peoples? The literary evidence now points strongly in this direction: The Jews, in fact, were not the colonizers of Canaan but the aboriginal people themselves, who although dominated by colonizing foreign cultures remained strong in their resistance to spiritual and cultural assimilation. They remained a people apart, as native cultures often remain to this day, with stronger spiritual ties to their lands than their conquering colonizers. Weinfeld goes on to show that sin and redemption are anchored in a relationship to the land—and to nature—that led to the original covenant.

Earlier in this century, in his provocative study of the origins of monotheism, Freud asked us to consider evidence that Moses was probably an Egyptian. In the same manner, I am suggesting that the evidence requires us to consider that the Hebrew tribes themselves were probably the native Canaanites of their pre-biblical time, exiles in their own land. And their drive to repossess the land assimilated every dispossessed people in the area.

Hebraic culture grew into an assimilating one, and as it acquired the written language that became archaic Hebrew, it reached out to Greek and other literatures, which it translated and transformed from cuneiform writing into the Hebrew alphabet. Weinfeld prefers the profound influence of Greek history on Israel, but the more penetrating influence remains the indigenous one, which in its drive to repossess and re-spiritualize the land, gathered in all who were exiled in their own land. That is why the history of King David, founder of the nation of

Israel, describes him with all the attributes of an indigenous spirit: of humble origins, a tender of flocks and orchards, a composer of songs, who would become leader of a band of what the Bible calls "outcasts"— his first army—who might have been merely aboriginals.

Who among the biblical writers could have composed such a dynamic portrait? J had written the story of a similarly dynamic personality in her portrait of Joseph, but David is more fully animated by indigenous roots, and his author, S, must himself have had close ties to the indigenous people. How did such a person, of native Canaanite background, receive such an exalted position at the court of Rehoboam, when this great work was written? We have come to the story of J and S.

3

J and S: Companions

If David was at least part aboriginal, and if he transmitted to the Jews his mother's *culture* if not her religion, then it was an exilic culture, the one held on to by the marginalized aboriginal Hebrews who did not join in the conquest or link up with the remaining Hebrew tribes.

But David stands for the new culture—even more than the religion Moses symbolized. What happened in the history of exile, the enslavement of some of the aboriginal Hebrews in Egypt, and in the dispossession of large areas by invading cultures? According to Weinfeld, this history was probably replaced by the story of the patriarchs in exactly the same way founding myths were established in Greek culture. J no doubt reveled in refining this mythic history, turning the great story-cycles of Jacob and Joseph into high art—until the lost land became the "promised land."

A little later, S was creating the new history of David's conquest, where memory of the old loss of the land was transformed into the poetry and history of a modern culture, buoyed by the new library David built in his palace. I first came across a sense of this vibrant new Hebraic culture during a research trip to Israel. As I noted in *The Lost Book of Paradise*, I met Professor Moshe Idel for lunch one day at the Hebrew University on Mt. Scopus. We speculated about prebiblical Jewish religion—a subject in which Idel's insights are notable—and about the independence of the early biblical historians and poets from religion. I asked him to accompany me to the new Mormon campus down the road, where tabletop models of the city of Jerusalem had been installed. Four models showed Jerusalem at different periods, and the one that drew me was the oldest: a representation of the City of David, the palaces with their archives and libraries standing, but the Temple not yet conceived.

The model, however, was disappointing, although we couldn't say exactly why. But one week later I found another model of Davidic Jerusalem that was being prepared for the David's Tower Museum. Where the Mormon model appeared empty and colorless, this one teemed with life, showing tiny figures and animals in the streets, including men sitting in the coffee shops that lined the famous street to the palace library. Shops of all kinds displayed their wares, including papyrus scrolls and writing implements.

I felt closer to home—to the reality of heritage as a home—when I found that street; it brought me closer to imagining myself alive at that time. And I could imagine what was within the nation's new library (its archives as well as texts and translations from other cultures, in clay, stone, papyrus, even skins) because I had previously envisioned the early authors themselves, in my translations for *The Book of J* and *A Poet's Bible,* where I had first detected as well the caravan trade in texts among far-flung civilizations.

The tiny figures sitting in the cafes outside the palace came alive: Among them would be many of the hundreds of court writers and archivists, arguing the latest translations and interpretations. I imagined one poet, having just returned from a visit to other libraries in Egypt or the Near East, recounting his or her finds there. Evidence of travel had abounded in the model: monkeys, parrots, heaps of spices, and even the "tea" they were drinking suggesting Africa, India, even farther. Caravans passed through Jerusalem regularly—how can we imagine a great writer not joining one, to visit foreign libraries, some just a few days' journey away?

At the same spot in Jerusalem today, on a clear afternoon, one may glimpse Tel Aviv on the coast; though scholars have shunned the thought, it is unlikely that a writer would sit out his or her entire life in a small town like Jerusalem.

A poet's training would also have required the translation of cuneiform texts into the new Hebrew alphabet. Poetic texts in Canaanite languages, set in clay or penned on papyrus, were already quite ancient. Even older, the classic poetic texts of Egypt and Mesopotamia would need retranslation. Can we imagine that Solomon himself did not try his hand at translating the Egyptian love poetry or Tamil love epics from India that bear such resemblance to his own Song of Solomon?

Even earlier, the major Near Eastern empire was translating archaic texts into cuneiform Hittite by the fifteenth century B.C. And by the time of Solomon's empire in the tenth century B.C., Phoenicians had translated the literary texts of Mycenaean Greece into their alphabet, a sister language to Hebrew. Hebraic poets may have worked from these translations in the Phoenician libraries, or they may have already made their own translations into archaic cuneiform Hebrew. A Jerusalem poet needed travel only to the coast to have access to Mycenaean Greek texts in an ancient palace library: Recent scholarship has confirmed this spectacularly, showing that the Philistines, or "sea people," were most likely colonizing Greeks.

No doubt J and S would have frowned upon the repression of parts of their texts that have been erased. Freud's concluding comment in *Moses and Monotheism* on the subsequent history of the biblical text is: "The distortion of a text is not unlike a murder. The difficulty lies not in the execution of the deed but in the doing away with the traces." What happens when the traces are hidden or conveniently lost is that we receive an anonymous text that wants to pretend that its authors actually erased their own names, like monks or nuns or devout self-flagellants. All the evidence shows that the authors were proudly known by their names during their lifetimes and wrote to win each other's esteem just as authors do today.

So what about the clichés concerning a biblical "tradition" or a "world of biblical literature"? These terms are routinely used to blind us to the way real writers work. They suggest that biblical authors wrote to fit into a tradition of the safely dead, when it is more likely they thrived among their living peers, as writers and artists always have. It is impossible today to imagine the emergence of an eminent American poet like John Ashbery without Frank O'Hara and his tragic early death. It is just as impossible to imagine Eliot without Pound and Yeats, or Hemingway without Gertrude Stein. In the same way, J and S wrote for each other and probably many other contemporaries, as Marlowe and Shakespeare wrote poetry for each other and with little concern for wider publication. It is almost equal to murder, as Freud suggests, when their names are hidden; it is a type of cultural obliteration that unseeing tradition imposes on the Solomonic culture, which produced great writers, and long before their priestly counterparts distorted the picture.

In *Moses and Monotheism*, Sigmund Freud demonstrates a way of reading that looks past conventional meanings and asks of a text the same depth of personality one would ask of a person. A person tells us his story, and yet as we come to know her or him we find that often there is much hidden behind it, sometimes unknown to our friend as well. Freud showed that the same respect must be paid to the complexity of classic texts—that they must not be read in their obvious homage but that we must put our desire for homage aside and treat the work as living tissue if we are to grow as readers. Of course, this is just what critics of Freud's book did not do; instead, they read the book at face value and failed to perceive that it is foremost a demonstration of self-critical investigation.

The current state of contemporary biblical scholarship is not dissimilar. For all the brilliance of academic readings, they remain surface insights because the scholars and critics themselves are unable to demonstrate any self-awareness commensurate with the text. Once upon a time, even Spinoza could recognize the original authors, but the modern industry of academic scholarship has varnished over the Court Historian so that we can see only the surface of the text, while the author is lost among competing theories about his didactic intentions. Is his narrative a moral work, a theological, political, or historical one? These conventional questions are applied equally to all of the text in the books of Samuel, serving to keep S's work inseparable. In such a context the largely literary purposes of S are reduced to incidents and episodes undifferentiated from David and Goliath, David and the Queen of Sheba, David and Saul, and the rest. Yet S's great work of art is not written for any of these purposes. We might just as well say that *Hamlet* and *War and Peace,* also works about love and war, were written to fulfill moral or political agendas.

In our time, however, there have been some notable American scholars who have been responsive to authorship (Robert Gordis, Harry Orlinsky, and H. L. Ginsberg among them), and I am lucky to have known them personally while they were alive. I regret having missed a chance to talk with the greatest of them, E. A. Speiser, who died in 1965. In probably the most important work of American biblical scholarship, the Genesis volume in the Anchor Bible series, Speiser writes, "J may well have been a contemporary of that other outstanding writer to whom we are indebted for the court history of David. Did the two, then, know each other personally? And if so, what were the relations between them?" Until now, the answers lay dormant, unimagined. The current generation of biblical scholars has shrunk in imaginative potency, and few have even acknowledged Speiser's questions. But Speiser provoked in me a desire to honor his work with a response, and to interpret the evidence that great writers of independent mind rarely exist in isolation.

There are exceptions, but the rule remains that great writers do not exist in a vacuum. They come in groups and in pairs, from Sophocles and Euripides, to Shakespeare and Marlowe, to Hawthorne and Melville, and in most cases they read, argue, stimulate, and respond to each other. Such is the most extraordinary case in the Bible, the apparent relationship between what scholars call the J writer of the Pentateuch and the Court Historian, or S writer of 2 Samuel. While scholars note the relationship between the two texts and the comparable literary qualities, they stop short of imagining the authors themselves. Why? The answer to this question lays bare the central taboo in biblical studies that continues to hide its source: an aversion to origins, and to imagining a living culture in all its diversity. A culture is far more than scribes and editors and religious officials writing in a dead language; it is fundamentally what we would today call a secular phenomenon, involving the arts and sciences of the time. So biblical scholars who are secular avoid the problem by repressing the notion of ancient culture with theories of redactors and didactic motivations ascribed to the original authors. Again, it is as if we erased all memory of Shakespeare as a man and read *Hamlet* as a moral or political document.

Yet times are changing and biblical scholarship is beginning to unthaw from the great freeze of imagination concerning the text. To cite a mundane but popular analogue, consider the difference in perception of indigenous American culture represented by the recent movie *Pocahontas* and the same legend a generation ago. Then, Native American culture was perceived as simple, clean, primitive; now it resonates an aura of complexity and state-of-the-art knowledge of the boundaries between culture and nature.

Even today some commentators refer to ancient Hebraic culture as primitive, directing their attention instead to ethical issues, for instance. They prefer to ignore the creative process while honoring the history of monotheism—as if written biblical art would be unworthy of standing beside secular Greek culture on its own merits. "Their most enduring legacy was their religion" (Margaret Oliphant, *The Atlas of the Ancient World*, 1992) is how the ancient Hebrews are typically described, implying that their creative culture can be dismissed in the same way European supremacists look down upon Asian and African cultures. But new issues raised by multiculturalism help to reveal that early Hebraic culture produced the Bible's great writers in the centuries before biblical religion dominated.

4

The Hebrews: An Indigenous History, Part 2

Considering the indigenous background of S as well as of David, new frontiers in science are showing how aboriginal cultures are less primitive than previously imagined. Paleobotany and ethnobotany join with archaeology to reveal that the agricultural and horticultural knowledge of aboriginal tribes is in many instances beyond our own. Native peoples farmed and managed whole forests that until recently we thought were wild. They studied plants and seeds we have not even discovered yet, producing a wide diversity of plant products. The image we used to hold of primitive "gatherers" is mostly wrong; "explorers" is more like it. Perhaps "professors of the forest" might be even more accurate. Their creative culture, as it lay in the tribal background of S, can be expected to be equally advanced.

It is likely that the later Hebrew tribes who founded the monarchy of Israel were not concerned with conquering their relatives, the "outcast" aboriginal peoples who lived beyond the Canaanite city walls. They did not possess fields for farming or large herds, but lived with their trees and vegetation, already displaced from their ancestral lands by the invading Canaanite cultures. In *The Territorial Dimension of Judaism* (1982), W. D. Davies emphasizes the subtext in biblical thought about "The Land of Israel as the place where Yahweh abundantly gave material gifts of all kinds to his people." Davies, being of the old school, has no questions about the founding myths of the patriarchs—such as recent revelations about how they were modeled on Greek myth. So Davies can write, "We encounter here that element in Israel's thought on The Land which it may have met before it settled in Canaan." Where did Israel live before that—and why assume it was ignorant about land? Davies has no answers, yet he provides a picture of Israel arriving in Canaan and meeting the local "primitives," who were more settled wanderers. The Hebrew tribes learned from these natives how they "could not conceive of a god as limited to one spot. The entire area which the god was considered to frequent became identified as his land, even though the first spot where he had manifested himself continued to be regarded as his home."

There it is: the seed for a God of Israel who subsumes all local gods. One step further, and this God may become Most High and Lord of the Earth. But the seed came from the native peoples, according to Davies, and were he more openminded, he might have recognized that these native peoples were the Hebrews themselves before they had mythologized their past. Again we meet the old prejudice against primitives, imagining them as nomadic and not a *cultivating* (hence cultivated) people. Yet they cultivated trees, vines, dates, nuts, olives—long before the settled Canaanites and their Baal religions, whom Davies considers more civilized. Baal and his pantheon were agricultural gods, tied to settled lands, which used to be thought of as the path to civilization.

Yet the crops farmed by the settled, foreign Canaanites were largely imported strains, as paleobotany can confirm today. The religions and cultures also came from foreign lands. It was the aboriginal people of Israel who provided the basis for an Israelite religion, as ethnobotany confirms in unraveling the complex role of the native shamans. These shamans were prophet and leader, musician and artist, translators of spirit, explorers of a consciousness of The Land. In short, an aboriginal Canaanite shaman was a likely model for King David.

David's marriages to aboriginal women, such as Abigail and Ahinoam, are related with great sensitivity in the books of Samuel. According to Eugene H. Maly in *The World of David and Solomon* (1966), Abigail "belonged to an influential Negeb tribe whose allegiance could mean much to the young outlaw." While Maly, a traditional exegete, uses the deadpan "mean much" to suggest political scheming, we now can surmise that it truly means much more. The years as an outcast were for David a powerful return to the oppressed culture of his mother: It was there, with aboriginal peoples, that he became more than a sweet singer. He becomes a strong poet, translating indigenous wisdom tied to dreams of the land into the psalms of the Bible: dreams of speaking to the creator of that land.

The tired old model of Hebraic biblical religion is also caught concisely by Maly. "Whereas the pagans [sic] needed constantly to have recourse to the mythological past into which they could fit the recurring pattern of the present, the Hebrews looked confidently to the future and saw the unexpected event of the present as a kind of divine preview of what would take place." It is a shame that prejudice against native cultures blinds Maly from valuing them—he resembles the worst kind of missionary here. In one fell swoop his idealization of Hebrew religion also wipes out any recognition of Hebraic culture. It is easier today to imagine a blend of these two—the misnamed "pagan" and the misunderstood "Hebrews"—and the character who best embodies them is David. The religion that suggests a mastery of history is instead the drama of David's experience in translating his knowledge of the land into a poetry of action and a poetry of thought. In S's sublime representation, David translates the unexpected event of the present into a confidence in the future.

A textbook history might begin this way:

Just seven or eight thousand years ago, before crop and livestock farming had begun to spread and with it an explosion in population density, the people of Canaan were still made up largely of indigenous tribes descended from the Stone Age. These were the aboriginal people who in a short time would become known as the Hebrew tribes. First, how-ever, they were to become exiles in their own land, displaced by the spreading civilizations based on agriculture.

The many nations described as Canaanites in the Bible—Edomites, Moabites, Ammonites, etc.—were not indigenous to Canaan but rather expanding peoples from the Fertile Crescent of Mesopotamia and the Middle East who were technologically advanced. They founded walled cities and cleared land for farming, pushing the aboriginal people to the margins. By the time we meet up with them in the Bible, they are described as the "outcasts" whom King David turned into an army that would defeat the Philistines (also an invading people, the "sea people" from the Mediterranean).

Nevertheless the indigenous Hebrews were more than nomadic hunters and gatherers; their gathering of fruit and nuts developed into a sort of farming at their origins, the cultivation of trees. They under-stood an early form of genetics that allowed cultivation of dates, figs, vines, and olives. And so they tended to live in settled sites, where their groves were planted. These aboriginal people, known originally as Natufian, lived in stone-house settlements as early as ten thousand years ago, and learned to cultivate their surrounding terrain.

Now, these people probably lived a pleasurable life. The trees offered an abundant and easy existence, and there was no pressure to expand—which is why we find even today that hunter-gatherers are loath to give up their lifestyles. The invention of agriculture no doubt came from a grimmer necessity, whether overpopulation or climatic changes. But earlier, these gathering societies displayed an enormous interest in art. In the earliest Stone Age, rock drawings and cave paint-ings are found everywhere, and in 1995 it was revealed that some of the greatest artists humanity has produced painted in the caves of southern France over 30,000 years ago. There is no doubt that their verbal arts were every bit as poignant, elaborate, and complex. Societies such as these were perhaps closer to happiness than most, and they found the relative leisure to explore the boundaries of their happiness in art.

Civilized agriculture changed everything. The immigrants and their expanding cities in Canaan during the Neolithic period pushed these aboriginal Hebrews to the margins. By David's time, they were known as "outcasts," since their settlements, like Native American encampments, were undefended by walls. Yet their culture remained rich in the arts of poetry and music.

Does this sound so unusual? Consider the Pygmy peoples of Africa, whose remnants today live the same hunter/gathering lifestyle. They are extraordinarily expert on every living thing in their environment, using herbs and roots to make medicines, and they understand all aspects of the plant life. They are also experts in ethology, the behavior of animals, which was perhaps less significant to the aboriginal Hebrews of Canaan, who had moved away from forests to create and tend their own groves of trees. Studies of the African Pygmy note two most unusual aspects of this Neolithic life: the parents' exceptional love for their children and their grand passion for a rich range of music and dance.

Over time, most indigenous people were assimilated into the Hebrew tribes we read about in the Bible. Yet many remained apart, even in David's time, and these were considered primitive. The position of Pygmies in Africa today might resemble the Hebrew aboriginals and the way they were used. "As far as possible, the cultivators make sure they remain unaware of the value of money, for fear they will become too expensive. In the opportune season, at least, the Pygmies do a lot of field work for them" (Cavalli-Sforza, *The Great Human Diasporas*, 1995). David spent many of his "lost years" among outcast people like these, and they were among his rebel band when he was on the run from Saul, according to the legends in 1 Samuel, written by lesser writers than S. These biblical passages suggest that David might have learned much from the outcast aboriginals about the joys of living in the present, not bound to the oppressive and polytheistic agricultural traditions now dominant in the land. Considering the Pygmies by analogy, Colin Turnbull, the first anthropologist to live with them, says they are invested in the present and free of burdensome pasts and indebted futures. He translates one of their sayings, which could have been a stanza of outcry in one of David's psalms: "If it is not here and now, then what do where and when matter?" Most important, what David learned from people like these, as portrayed by S, are the arts of life and poetry.

The figure of David portrayed by S is built on a character who pushes the boundaries of living in the present—and who, not incidentally, is a master of the arts of poetry, music, and no doubt dance as well. He fits a certain Neolithic stereotype of the man who pushes the boundaries of art in life, as in poetry and music. In his own civilized culture, he transformed the arts of these indigenous peoples into the psalms for which he became renowned. He also transformed the idea of leadership, modeled on the shaman artist, into a messianic basis for great renaissances of the future.

By the time the aboriginal Hebrew tribes returned from slavery in Egypt, they found their compatriots pushed to the limits by invading cultures, from the Philistines to the east, the Moabites and Ammonites to the west, and the Aramites to the north. Many of the indigenous Hebrews left behind had assimilated among the invaders or become marginalized. But the return of the exiles galvanized the larger population who had remained unconquered in Canaan, so that the "conquest" of Israel could begin. Over several hundred years, this history would become blended into a single story of exile and return—for even those left behind in Canaan had been thrown into exile from their ancestral territories by the foreigners.

5

A Biography of Monotheism

S's narrative has been commonly called a history by critics who deny the imaginative powers of a great author. Some, recognizing those powers, have called it a novella, or even the first great novel. But none has been brave enough to admit that it is most likely only part of a greater work that has been expunged. Yet when the author's identity has been guessed at, he is always characterized as a court functionary, a historian or political apologist. It is only logical, then, that this great artist wrote not simply a novel or history but a new genre in poetic prose: a creative biography of more than a man, a biography that revealed his essence, his transformative powers. In his life of David, S portrays a culture based on an individual God and an individual man in his image.

Could monotheism have been represented in a more compelling way than in a biography? Having read what his mentor, J, had done with the life of Moses, S has played off her portrait of a prophet of singular mind to reveal a king of boundless sensibility, a true subject of biography. Yet, as S learned from J as well, David's true character is an image of Yahweh, and in this tension between bounded man and unbounded God—at the boundary, as it were, between life and death— we receive a biography of Yahweh. We are made to feel Yahweh's necessary singularity, his love for David and his land, as the essence of monotheism.

A prominent critic of the Court Historian, David M. Gunn, in *The Story of King David* (1978), tempts controversy and calls S's book an entertainment, which he defines quite wonderfully as demanding "the active engagement of those being entertained, which challenges their intellect, their emotions, their understanding of people, of society and of themselves." That said, Gunn cannot bring himself to imagine that the author intended it so! Instead, he cringes from his own surmise by asserting that "the author believed himself to be recounting in essence what actually happened, whether or not it was precisely what happened. Certainly the story is narrated with a firm feeling for actuality." Here is a scholar who cannot imagine that an author who created what he describes as a work of art could have been conscious of it. Instead, like most scholars, Gunn projects his naive views of the primitive back onto an author who he imagines could write only a "traditional story," by which he means saga history.

Gunn's problem is a paradigm for biblical scholarship: He can speculate about differing genres but he cannot imagine genre-*bending*, which is what most great writers do. Great writers like S and J stretch the genre, and the critic must be able to imagine this and sense the play of irony. But irony is too often a foreign country to scholars.

Gunn also makes comparisons among similar words used by S and J, noting the differing contexts. But there is no sense of the play involved—or of a living contact between writers. Instead, the pathetic fallacy of authors writing in a vacuum—called "tradition"—is invoked, as it is in the dubious phrase "a world of biblical literature," employed by some other critics.

At the end of a book purporting to argue the origins and growth of the Bible, David Damrosch, in his influential study *The Narrative Covenant* (1987), writes that the words were written by "authors whose greatest ambition was to disappear into their text." Although this wish may apply to the redactors, editors, and scribes, it is a mistake that many postmodernist critics make when they assume the greatest writing was penned by men who worship at the idol of a text as critics do. Damrosch may imagine some kind of monkish idealism at work in the authors, but it is disingenuous of him, especially after comparing their work to Shakespeare, among other Elizabethan allusions. Yes, there is a sense in which the actor Shakespeare disappears into his drama, and perhaps the writer Shakespeare was not overly concerned with how his literary obituary might read, but the only way he might be said to vanish into his text is as a hugely ambitious artist. The same no doubt holds true for J and S, among many of the great biblical progenitors. Besides, the weight of contextual and comparative studies shows that the early biblical authors were renowned in their day.

At the midway point of his book, by way of contrast to J's unknown political attitudes, Damrosch writes, "Shakespeare's attitudes toward English history, for example, are variously reconstructed." And yet, do Shakespeare's political attitudes really explain anything about the greatness of his art? Shakespeare's "social agenda," if we can speak for a moment like these voguish biblical critics, was to interact with a living culture and his contemporary colleagues in the arts, as I will show is equally true of J and S. We can be fairly certain that Shakespeare did not spend the better part of his energy on political historians.

It is no more likely that J was either "consolidating a new religious and social order" or "trying to recreate a distant past as a way to understand what went wrong," as Damrosch asserts. Like most academic biblical scholars, he can only imagine a writer who fills a social need. Yet J, as well as S, writing at the son of Solomon's grand court, is writing to engage and shape a living culture, and not to satisfy a social agenda.

To what extent, then, can we say S's court history is a biography of monotheism, or what we may call an artistic novel? S writes an artful realism, creating scenes the reader knows he did not witness. "It happens one late afternoon that David rises from his bed, takes a walk around the palace roof, and from there, his glance falls upon a woman in her bath." Yet in fact there is abundant irony, only deadpanned, and so what may earn the designation of novel is its self-conscious art. Our anxiety with the term *novel* may have to do with the sense of who it is written for, who is to be entertained. Let's ask the question of S: Is it the priests who are the primary audience for the story of David, or any group of devotees? Unlikely. Is it the court, then, a group of extended family, courtiers, diplomats, and educated traders—a group of perhaps no more than a thousand potential living readers? It would appear so, especially when we consider how expensive it was to make many copies of the text. The court would have had to subsidize its publication, yet among the readers there must have been a desire for growth and self-knowledge that also embraced self-criticism.

Entertainment? And yet, is not a sermon's place in the liturgy often a time to entertain the congregation? Yes, there is the moral instruction as well, though one might argue the same for certain artistic novels, especially the exercise in self-knowledge. But the best way to understand this great novel's purpose is to imagine the court writers and translators, an audience of perhaps no more than a hundred, all of whom are seeking a fresh paradigm in written literature around which to nourish a new culture. By this time, however, the court has approached the third generation after David and has become somewhat experienced and skeptical—an audience of hard critics. It would take a master like J— and her protégé, S—to disarm them. S's biography of monotheism might well have proven a deeply moving experience for them.

Compared to the seeming realism of S's work, the heightened realism of the New Testament Gospels do not hide a self-conscious irony but actually suppress authorship beneath a conscious awe of the purely autobiographical account. In place of the author's dynamic sensibility is supernatural portent. Instead of a turn toward writing, the Gospels turn away from it to a community of faith. In the post-Solomonic days of S and J, however, we sense "the fragmentary and fallen nature of human experience after the collapse of community and faith, and, as a counterbalance, the turn toward writing with its mythic possibilities." Written about the collapse of the Judeo-Greek assimilating culture of the Hasmonean Jews by John Dominic Crossan in *Who Killed Jesus?* (1995) these words could apply as well to the assimilating culture of David and Solomon's time a millennium earlier, when after Solomon's death it began to shrink back into itself, turning away from translation of the old traditions.

Yet no life of Jesus would have been likely without a prior life of David. Where Yahweh's beloved, David, embodied the range of human experience, Jesus transcends them; instead of testing the limits of Yahweh's love, he tests his subjects in a kingdom of belief. Reality has become literal, so that the literal-minded reader will find "mistakes" in the Gospels, and it is first some Jews who offer this critique, having lost the sense of authorship behind their own gospel of David. David's mistakes were plainly in view yet embraced in a loving reality, a paradigm of *chesed*, or lovingkindness.

The conventional critics today have turned the text into an idol: They recognize that S's David is imaginative but read it as if it were real. Yet S expands the representation of outward reality to include an interior one, and critics have a hard time understanding this because they resist walking in the shoes of the author and imagining his point of view. Instead of authors, they refer to "sources," and instead of a culture of writers, they refer to "redactors"—in other words, not creative writers but conformist men of scholastic minds like themselves.

6

A Sublime Burial of the Past

What may be the most important book of biblical scholarship in decades is the Israeli scholar Moshe Weinfeld's *The Promise of the Land* (1993). Weinfeld has been known throughout his career for his work on the Deuteronomic school of authors and editors. In addition to the underlying D author of Deuteronomy, this grouping includes others responsible for additions and emendations to many books of the Bible. Writing many centuries after J and S had died, the Deuteronomists worked to ensure that the great authors would be forgotten. They rewrote the history of Israel from a limited religious perspective, downplaying the poets and authors descending from David's and Solomon's courts. The self-aware literary strategies of J and S are forgotten, along with the court culture that nourished them and responded to their wit.

Weinfeld probed behind the "Promised Land" history of Israel, as it was reshaped by the Deuteronomists: priestly authors who reshaped many biblical books in addition to Deuteronomy, in the sixth century B.C.—more than three centuries after David and Solomon. In the older sources of that time, Weinfeld found a surprising conversion of Greek literary strategies into Hebraic form. And one of these involved a divine promise of land. Weinfeld has inherited Freud's insight into the Bible: The more that religion sublimates the physical world, as Deuteronomy does, the greater the repression of the past. Any trace of memory about the aboriginal origins of the Hebrew tribes would now be submerged in the mythic histories of the patriarchs and stories of the Promised Land—in other words, in the writings of J and S.

Praising Weinfeld's latest work, David N. Freedman, co-editor of *The Archaeology of the Bible,* writes that "one of the most pressing controversial issues of our own time" is how the Bible deals with the land. What is odd about this statement is that the pressing issue in Weinfeld's book is not the relevance to *our* time but to ancient days. Even though the Freudian implications about how the Promised Land came to be a central story are understated, Weinfeld's imaginative reconstruction of the past is rare in biblical thought. Rarer still is his evocation of the biblical writers—and the suggestion that they fashioned a covering myth for their true origins in the story of the Promised Land. J wove her own version of that story into the Book of Exodus, yet she as well as S seem fully aware that it is mythic. They are more focused upon human relationships to the land than supernatural promises.

Freud marshaled nineteenth-century biblical scholarship to show how two strands of Hebrew history diverged, one going down to Egypt and at times becoming enslaved, and another remaining in the land of Canaan. Of these two, Freud finds the Egyptian emigrants the more interesting, especially the sophisticated Egyptian influence of their leader, Moses. It had not occurred to me that the indigenous Hebrew tribes left behind in Canaan might be the truer poets.

"If Moses were an Egyptian," Freud begins *Moses and Monotheism,* and soon many enigmas in the Bible begin to make a new sense. We understand how the story of Moses's abandonment among the papyrus reeds is an archetypal hero's myth in many cultures, and how it was necessary to provide a covering myth for his Egyptian education. "If the Jews were an aboriginal people in Canaan" is how Weinfeld's work might have begun, for soon many mysteries about the Hebraic obsession with the spirit of the land begin to make better sense.

If the Hebraic culture includes more aboriginal influences than it acknowledges, then we must consider how much has been lost in the editing process of the Bible over the centuries by religious authorities. During the Hebraic renaissance of David and Solomon, the indigenous influences behind David's psalms, for instance, would have been apparent. But already the sophistication of the Hebrew Bible embodies the cultural wish to transform this past. The desire to bury aboriginal origins altogether may have won out in just a century after the Hebraic renaissance, as court life disintegrated and the religious cult consolidated its influence. Civilizations create mythic origins for themselves, but rarely does an advanced one tolerate a primitive association. And aboriginal peoples, then as now, are mistakenly viewed as primitive.

No other culture in history more resembles an indigenous one than that of the Hebrews. Building on the latest scholarship, it has become clear to me that the literary sophistication of the Hebrew Bible is based on the cultural wish to bury this past. The Hebraic renaissance of David and Solomon was accompanied by the will to play down the humble, aboriginal origins of the Jewish people. It's natural enough. All civilizations create mythic origins for themselves—then, as now, aboriginals are viewed as primitive, and no advanced civilization would want a primitive label attached to itself. The ancient Egyptians and Greeks and even Phoenicians were not going to respect a civilization of aboriginals, any more than Brazil or Australia today respect theirs.

Can a renaissance bury the past? The origins of the Bible in the biblical writers of David and Solomon's time is most likely a renaissance, the Jews having recovered an earlier period in which they were at home in their land. In the third millennium B.C., cultures from the east were invading Canaan, continuing into the second millennium, when the Philistines and Hittites followed, pushing some of the Hebrew tribes to the margin while others fled to Egypt, only to become enslaved at some point. At the time around 1000 B.C., when they formed a monarchy of their own, the Hebrew tribes from Egypt had returned and been absorbed among those who had won much of their land back from the foreign invaders that are imprecisely called Canaanites by tradition. It was in Israel's interest to make them seem a settled unity in order to create a powerful tale of conquering the land.

The tale is not a lie; it is actually a strong sublimation of the truth, which is that the Hebrews had become exiles in their own land—in much the position Native Americans find themselves in today. Just as those tribes are trying to restore their culture, the Hebrews began their drive to a renaissance about the time that Abraham was supposed to have arrived in Canaan from the cosmopolis of Ur.

In Abraham, Hebraic myth had a representative from the dominant advanced culture of the time, Mesopotamian, and a mythic tapestry with which to veil its indigenous origins. As we read J's story in Genesis of the arrival in Canaan of the patriarchs and on up to Joseph's education in Egypt—importing Egyptian sophistication as well—we are absorbing the archetypal foundation myths that pre-Roman and archaic Greek colonies created many centuries before. Even the stories of Jacob come from foreign sources, "adopted by the Israelites and incorporated into their national history"—until J writes them into the Bible so that Jacob the trickster may echo the uncanniness of an indigenous shaman.

We are introduced to the evidence by Weinfeld: "The genre of foundation stories consists of two parts: the first part describes the migration of the ancestor, and the second describes the settlement. In contrast to Joshua the settler, Abraham is a wanderer. . . . Just as Aeneas is the first ancestor of the nation, 'the pater,' and not the first settler, so is Abraham 'the father'—and not, like Joshua, the conqueror and settler."

Weinfeld offers many other examples, from naming to apportionment by tribe to the founding of a temple: "In Israel as in Greece, we find that priority was given to the erection of a temple on the site of the new settlement and to the division of the land among the tribes by means of divine lot." The thrust of the evidence goes to the precedent of a "promised land": "The most surprising analogy is between the promise of the land to the Greek settlers by Apollo and to the Israelite settlers by Yahweh." In fact, all the "civilizing" conventions concerning the land, from the dispossession of the Canaanites in J's Pentateuch to the submission of peoples and kings during the wars of David in S's 2 Samuel, are modeled on archaic sources, according to Weinfeld. The Moabites, the Edomites, the Aramaeans—they become "tributary vassals of David," one of numerous phrases S has lifted out of ancient literature and woven into the Hebrew Bible.

Gone is the memory that these same Moabites, Edomites, and Aramaeans were foreign invaders in Canaan buried with bitter memory of losing the land. The aboriginals are never mentioned except by S, who remakes them into Israel's salvation as the "outcasts" who join with David to solidify his army. And the foundation culture of the Hebrew aboriginals has become transformed at its height by S into David's restoration of the land and singing of psalms: a Hebraic culture with room as well for accepting the gift from its creator of a promised land. In the same way, J had provided the precedent for S in creating a new genre to enfold the old stories, a poetic prose that brings the characters to startling life.

In J's Genesis there is no thought yet of inventing a history in which the Canaanites are "exterminated" (as is suggested centuries later in Deuteronomy). The term J employs is not even "expel"—it is "inherit from." But how could the Israelites inherit the land from the foreign Canaanites who dispossessed *them* in the past? In a grand sublimation, they inherit the land instead in a promise extracted from Yahweh.

By the time the exiled Hebrew tribes returned from ancient Egypt, they may no longer have identified with the tribes left behind, some of whom probably assimilated among the conquering Canaanites while others became marginalized. There was a need for redefining the land from which they were pushed out, of redefining their exile—the Exodus and the Promised Land are the sublime result. Connected by moral ties, a theological dimension to the land is always present in aboriginal culture. It is theirs not to possess but to care for and preserve. Take it away—and they are not merely dispossessed and outcasts but their culture suffers a loss of meaning. Since the land is more than a homeland but a sacred trust, to forget it—to stop caring for it—would be a sin. This is evident today in indigenous ecology, to the point where we find many dispossessed Native American tribes who are devoted to teaching how to care for the land, and whose redemption is foreseen in their ability to care for it better than invaders like ourselves.

We can find the same spiritual transformations in early Jewish religion. The foundation of the Sabbath, for instance, and the Sabbatical and Jubilee years of leaving the land unworked, originally had ties with resting the land and resting from working it. To hold possession of the land required a moral fitness, an ethical behavior—ethics too were derived from the land itself, as in aboriginal culture. In the later poets of the Bible, the prophets, ethical injustices are punishable by exile. In Amos or Isaiah, exile is the most profound punishment there is, and it is easy to imagine why the early Hebrew tribes who remained behind and were conquered by Canaanites would rather have assimilated than go down to Egypt—the fear of exile was stronger than the fear of slavery.

It may become evident now how David's transformations of indigenous poetry into psalms—and S's transformation of aboriginal vitality into David's character—were necessary frames for a renaissance culture based on the power of writing. They gave their writing the spiritual dimension of an equal footing with Yahweh, a dialogue with him that Martin Buber called the I/thou relationship—and which is manifest in the covenant. Yahweh's desire for the kind of loyalty that S calls "lovingkindness" in 2 Samuel, and is further spiritualized later by the prophets, is similar to what we know today if we imagine the creator as an embodied, life-evolving ecosystem. We have learned that a healthy ecosystem requires ethical living, and a "disloyalty" to the ecosystem results in the extinction or exile of its life. Ultimately, we find in Weinfeld that "observing the laws of resting the land is, according to the priestly sources, a necessary condition for dwelling in the land."

The Canaanite conquerors were probably viewed as polluters of the land and so could not have truly inherited it. Later, it is only a short step to a spiritualizing of the land that in Deuteronomy is connected with the full range of ethical sins. The imagery of a devastated ecosystem— of turning the land into a "wasteland"—is used as a figure of punishment. In Hosea, dishonesty no less than murder leads to "that the earth is withered, everything that dwells on it languished," and this imagery is developed to poetic heights in Isaiah, where "the earth dries up and withers, the whole world withers and grows sick" because the ethics of the covenant with Yahweh is violated. Here is the aboriginal tie to the land in all its great, shamanistic spirituality.

Finally, Weinfeld reminds us that "no other people in the history of mankind was as preoccupied as the people of Israel with the land in which they lived. The whole biblical historiography revolves around the Land." The spirit of the land has entered the people—so the aboriginal cultures understand it. They can never assimilate its loss, and the feeling of exile from it remains through millenniums. In the same way, the repressed connection to the land in Hebraic culture remained hidden until this century, when farmers returned to the land in Ottoman and British Palestine, forming kibbutzim, or farming cooperatives. What more resembles the lifestyle of aboriginal tribes than the unique manifestation of Israeli kibbutzim early in this century! As we find among Indians in the Amazonian rain forest today, or among the Pygmy tribes in the African rain forests, the spirit of shared work and resources is fundamental, and the idea of personal "possessions" is alien.

My own university writing instructor, the South African and English novelist Dan Jacobson, wrote a book about the Deuteronomic concept of a promised land, *The Story of the Stories* (1982), but without examining the *repressed* story of the writers themselves, I'm afraid. His lack of Hebrew scholarship probably kept him from realizing that many layers of biblical writing were strewn like varnish over the great transformations created by the J and S writers. Nevertheless, he always set before me the principle of digging for the hidden elements, just as he imbibed it from Freud's *Moses and Monotheism*. He writes, "We take it for granted that any story which enthralls us, from a little fairy tale like 'Cinderella' to a great tragedy like *Oedipus the King*, owes some of its power to hidden or obscured elements which help to determine the direction it takes." Jacobson's deduction that the Promised Land is a fiction remains true, yet what we see now is how crucial it is to understand why this fiction was created—and by whom. It was created not foremost by politicians and historians and priests but by writers like Jacobson himself, who had the creative powers to hide their indigenous sources without destroying them. That aboriginal power remains a love for the mothering land—and life-evolving ecosystem—in the prose and poetry of J and S to this day.

Three centuries after Solomon had died, the idols of his hundreds of foreign wives remained standing in Jerusalem, assimilated into a Hebraic culture that reminds one of the cultural plurality in Israel today. I believe that the aboriginal impulse was also largely ambivalent about the idol worship of the agricultural civilizations and instead devoted to the unbound spirit of the land. The prohibitions against idolatry that run through the Bible would thus appear to be a sublimation of indigenous spirit. Why the explanation centuries later, in the Prophets and Deuteronomists, that Israel's exile from the land into Babylon was a punishment for making covenants with Canaanites and honoring their gods? The answer should now be apparent: The Canaanites were foreigners in the land and the godly representation of spirit for the Israelites was the land itself.

Finally, there is an abhorrence of violence (though its necessity is understood) in aboriginal creativity also. Consider what J wrote in Genesis 4:11–13:

🌱 14   (*Book of J*)
        "What have you done?" he said. "A voice—your brother's
        blood—cries to me from the earth. And so it be a curse:

the soil is embittered to you. Your brother's blood sticks in its throat.

"You may work the ground but it won't yield to you, its strength held within. Homeless you will be on the land, blown in the wind."

Illusion and Fidelity

Comparison of the Abrahamic and Davidic covenants shows that both were bestowed as gifts upon individuals who served their masters—in this case, Yahweh—with the loyalty of lovingkindness. Here we find J and S at play, as her Abram (who needs to become an Abraham) is a creative transformation of a Greek foundation myth, becoming the founder of a religion. "Religions do need founders," Harold Bloom asserted in *The Book of J*, "even as strong literary works need authors. 'Oral traditions' do not compose works of aesthetic shape and value." And I interpret the work of another notable critic, Northrup Frye, to show that "oral traditions" are a myth conjured by scholars to cover up the origins of a written tradition they do not know how to acknowledge, since the memory of it has been distorted by pious scholarship itself.

So how does S's David play against J's Abram in their great narratives? As Abram founds the religion on Greek models, David founds the culture of biblical writers on indigenous models. Both of their characters move in a secular world, and neither J nor S is a religious writer like D, the Deuteronomist, or P, the priestly author. J takes Yahweh for granted and S relegates him to the background like a stern but doting mother figure.

In J's literary footsteps, S brings paleo-Hebraic poetry into a freshly modern world through David's psalms. Just as significantly, both J and S have transformed the mythic writing of other cultures into a creative prose that frames history and myth with a human context. Their prose is rooted in the personalities of male and female characters who reflect the image of a creative Yahweh, one who responds to lovingkindness. And the primary character for both writers was David, whose demonstrations of lovingkindness—whose grace and chivalry—was mirrored in many of J's characters, foremost in Joseph and Tamar.

The Judaic scholar Martin Buber was aware of the biblical authors' power as mythographers, which he analyzed in the "situating dialogues" between their characters and Yahweh. Buber was less interested in understanding the human drama of the writers themselves, which are woven into the stances or frames they create for the stories. The written frames that J and S provide for the Bible, a human and ironic distance from mythic situations, for the first time on the world's stage allow an acceptance of loss without religious submission.

Loss is borne with courage and charm by David, who suffers the worst losses a mature adult can know: a parent's loss of beloved children. David, in S's portrait, shows us more than how to mourn; he shows us how to continue our lives with an intensified appetite for love. David shows love of life in all his actions, but none more compelling than in his spoken words themselves, as imagined by S, and in his very writing— the psalms—many of them most likely penned by S as well. When his conscience is awoken, David frames loss with love.

David's psalms transmit the spirit of aboriginal poetry by honoring diversity, accepting the widest range of experience and emotion, from loving awe to ruin. By contrast, the normative tradition of biblical criticism reduces David's greatness of heart to the conventional. We may even say that the normative tradition today is anti-Hebraic, outside the inspired realm of transforming genres and traditions that characterized the Solomonic renaissance and produced J and S.

Perhaps the greatest transformative frame created by J and S is the illusion of spoken dialogue. Historians have been known to actually believe that the words S creates for David are historical—and that belief may be the measure of S's greatness as an artist. He makes history look easy to write, just as he makes the psalms appear to be transcribed from the poet's mouth. Again, this is the illusion of art, and it is so powerful that the normative biblical tradition once actually believed that this was oral poetry. In the same manner, it has been believed that the prose written by J and S had to have been based upon an oral tradition, and this conventional but blind approach is still being taken.

Illusion and fidelity—these are the hallmarks of great art, and we find them even on the walls of caves in prehistoric France 30,000 years ago, where a great paleo-artist created the illusion of a stampeding rhinoceros in long-ago Europe. Though he is conscious of the illusion of spokenness, S shows us a fidelity to reality—just as the paleo-artist did—that transforms into enchanting art our natural fear of life's raw power to defeat us. It is our awareness of the play between words and thought and music that creates the frame for the artist, permitting his own self-conscious creation of an illusion of spoken voices.

In the indigenous poems that inspired S there is a different frame. In place of the self-conscious poet is the illusion of a frameless nature itself: The primitive poem speaks directly to the elements. As far as the eye can see are the walls of this poet's house—in a rain forest Indian stilt house there are no windows, and no doors to muffle the songs of bird and ancestor monkey. The boundary between culture and nature—between self and feeling—remains transparent. S closed this transparent window and shifted attention to the self speaking and the creator hearing, yet the boundless space remains when a creator could hear one anywhere.

For David, S created the frame as well of the city of Jerusalem—*his* city. Jerusalem becomes a window to the land, and a shelter from the old loss of the land, the exile that is now being transformed into a dynamic culture. Now Jerusalem assimilates foreign cultures the way the aboriginal culture had assimilated nature. But the old loss is not buried; instead, it is incorporated into the spirit of the Bible. David can weep openly for his son Absalom—and for himself and his own pain—in a psalm to Yahweh. There is a restoration of the land as well in the image of a mothering Yahweh, fond of her charge's exuberant love of life.

There is something both messianic and shamanistic about David as the poet of psalms. His transformations are a shaman's art, but as the transformer himself, present in his poems as the speaker, the context is created for timelessness, a speaking across the ages in art—just as the shaman spoke directly to eternal spirits. David becomes the messianic model for Judaism, and even for Christianity, precisely because he is a poet. And, I would add, because his mother—as well as the writer S's mother—was an aboriginal princess. For S's mother, for that possibility, we have Solomon's love of diversity to thank, his ambition to honor his father David by assimilating a wide range of cultures.

So S provides David, in his great prose narrative, with a life that is messianic in its mirroring of Yahweh. David is represented with boundless appetite, boundless vision, and an awareness of his limitations as well. Just as he could not control the loss of his son Absalom, Yahweh cannot control David's appetite and must accept a mother's consolation for his imperfect protégé. Yet the founding of a culture is the paradigm for the creator's founding of nature, and David's founding of a Hebraic culture in Jerusalem is a restoration of ties to the land. Jerusalem will become a symbol of inexhaustable love, of ties as natural and as erotic as to a forest. To mirror that forest, David creates a palace with a library at its center, long before building a temple.

In S's perspective, David restores the outcast in his framing of a new tradition. His appetite for life breaks what seemed a natural bond with a past based on loss. But an irrepressible bond with our parents whispers, "If it was good enough for them, it is good enough for me." It's a wish to identify with origins, our parents serving as an elementary link to ultimate origins. To break this tradition is to become self-conscious and outside of it—outcast, if you will. David makes of being an outcast a new definition of nature, a *human* nature.

8

Mothers

We are just beginning to learn more about our own misconceptions of aboriginal people as we discover the evolutionary history of our species. David's nature, in the context of S's narrative, shares surprising characteristics with how ecologists describe ecosystems. At the same time, ethnobotany shows that aboriginal people have a cultural understanding of how ecosystems work. Two of the general principles that shape the ecosystem are the function of diversity and the function of sexual selection. Compare the functions of David's character. There is the diversity of his desires, his mistakes, his guile, his diverse interests, feelings, and loyalties—the diversity of his personality. And there is the importance of sexual selection, from his coupling with Bathsheba to the problems with Michal. Later tradition tends to suppress the vitality of David's diverse character and sexuality. But it remains vital in S: a freedom to explore what is natural, such as sexual boundaries, and make his own mistakes.

Recent developments in ecology describe the ecosystem as a context of complexity that frames what we still don't know about evolution: It is a structural mystery. David moves in his Hebraic culture as if he were in an ecosystem, in a complex mystery. In this natural-seeming structure—a mysterious culture—S can play with the illusion of history just as David in his psalms plays with the illusion of real speech.

Who wrote David's psalms? Some of them were probably written by S, the artist who penned his life and put the words in David's mouth in 2 Samuel. Just as a prayer or psalm follows S's narrative in the text—this one by another author—I believe that S's psalms were later separated from his original composition and became the core of the Book of Psalms. So it is S—or both David and S—who imbibed a poetry of indigenous lullabies at his mother's breast, and who composed the complex transformations of aboriginal poetry that set a new standard—for Hebrew poetry and for prayer.

There are studies of Canaanite literature in which it is compared to the Hebraic, but in most cases the differences rather than the similarities are what move us. The fundamental contrast arises because these Canaanite cultures seem foreign to the land, having first developed elsewhere, largely in the Fertile Crescent. The Hebrew poetry of the psalms absorbs the aboriginal culture with roots in the land, and our need to imagine the author S begins here. Without him, we are at a loss to describe what is unique about the psalms as well as his narrative in 2 Samuel.

The complexity in aboriginal poems stems from a direct translation of natural sources. Instead of framing with description and context, the poems embody the characteristics of nature as in a dream. A composition is made even more complex by the absence of self-consciousness. When S and J lend this quality to their texts, it is as a further source of clarifying and framing. Their self-consciousness takes the form of a distance from their characters. In a psalm especially, there is the sense of the speaking narrator in his distance from others and from Yahweh.

Yet the consciousness of the land is indispensable. Consider Psalm 8:

Yahweh Most High
your name shines
on the scroll of the world

from behind the lights
covering the heavens—
my lips like infants

held to the breast
grow
to stun the darkest thoughts

when I look up
from the work of my fingers
I see the moon and stars

your hand set there
and I can barely think
what is a man

how did you spare a thought for him
care to remember
his line

descending through death
yet you let him rise
above himself, toward you

held by music of words . . .
you set his mind in power
to follow the work of your hand

laying the world at his feet
all that is nameable
all that changes through time

from canyons to the stars
to starfish
at bottom of the sea

all that moves blazing a path
in air or water
or deep space of imagination on marked leather

Yahweh Most High
your name shines
on the scroll of the world.

Did David write this himself? It is easier to imagine that S wrote it, as it reflects his skill in creating David's dialogue in the Book of David. By framing psalms for David's hand, S transforms the love of naming land and sky into a self-consciousness of his own power as an artist, scratching this psalm on the leather skins he may have used for his scrolls. I have had to transform the imagery myself in translation, to remain true to the vitality of the original. But S's transformations are the crucial ones. His aboriginal model probably had the sun in the place of Yahweh, and instead of singing to his maker, the indigenous poet directly sang the praises of the world under the sun.

S, through his embodiment of David, has transformed our con-sciousness of creation through his own self-consciousness as a creator. Nevertheless, the mark of a native original is strong, as the psalm is quite different from the Canaanite treatment of the creator, Baal—especially in its love for the natural world.

Yet where would the creative spark to make such a profound transformation have come for S? No doubt his confidence would have been strengthened by J, who herself may have transformed the Song of Solomon, based on Solomon's own model. But the Song of Solomon does not embody a consciousness of its creator as the psalms do. Could S have been inspired by David himself, who transcribed the lullabies of his youth and the poems he encountered during his years with the outcasts? Yes, but still there is a new world in these psalms, a poetry that makes personal what used to be the exclusive power of the shamanistic world.

I have come to the conclusion that S's mother must have been a shaman herself, and passed this art down to her son in the manner of all such masters. That is the reason S was recognized as a prodigy and brought to J's attention. In replacing S's mother as his mentor, J taught him the transforming powers that would yield his great art.

Imagine S's written sources. In the palace library he would have found many old scrolls about the pre-Davidic period, scrolls about David's ancestors and youth—such as the Book of Ruth, which has survived—and court documents from David's time. From all of these he might have lifted telling details that become ironic when retold in the context of his court history. My colleague Harold Bloom was quick to backlight J in his comments about S in *The Book of J*, where he wrote, "J's marvelous contemporary is not primarily a comic and ironic writer, as she was, but his sophistication matches her acute consciousness of paradox." S's David may not seem as ironic a character as J's Yahweh because he is confined to the human, but within those confines he is continually surprising us with what appear to be extreme actions. Whether it is the sudden disappearance of grief when his son by Bathsheba is pronounced dead, or the interminable grief that Absalom causes, the narrative leads us to accept that David's actions are sagacious—and it is our very willingness to accept it, awed by the dimensions of this David, that is ironic, an irony S most exploited in many satisfying ways.

Nevertheless, Bloom does not miss the interplay between J and S, or fail to observe "the many complex crosscurrents passing back and forth between the Book of J and 2 Samuel." He compares Joseph's many-colored coat with the princess Tamar's, noting that both become emblems of cruelty. Bloom also notes that the young Joseph in J's text is described in a similar manner to David when he first comes to Saul. In a larger sense, both David and Joseph charm Yahweh, and Bloom describes J's Joseph as "Davidic." Yet J's women are even more like David—simply by the irony of their being drawn with more vitality than their husbands and sons. J's Tamar impels her way into the center of J's story—and becomes the ancestor of David, whose uncanniness in S's narrative she resembles (she also stands in for David's unnamed mother). J and S are at play here on many levels.

Yet it is Yahweh whom Bloom casts as J's counterpart to S's David. For both, "everything that matters most is perpetually new." That is, they possess an interior life that we witness by contrast to their movement from one border of experience to the next, leaving us hopeful yet anxious about what will come next.

J's narrative ends with the death of Moses, who dies an exile. David's death begins in effect with his loss of Absalom, who appears to represent David's mother by the power of his attachment. In the end, David is also a kind of exile from his mother's culture, the one that made him a poet and the symbolic founder of Israel's culture. In his transforming of an aboriginal poem into a psalm, as we shall see, David began the process of losing his mother. It makes sense that S portrays this sense of estrangement in David's passing, a sense that Solomon has already lost too much of David's heroic sensibility. For both J and S know themselves that already their work will be lost, as they are visibly losing their audience in the inexorable shrinking of Solomon's inheritance.

A typical estimation of how David's story is written is given by a noted biblical scholar, Walter Brueggemann, in his book *David's Truth*

(1985). Brueggemann describes S's accomplishment as giving David a "personal interiority" which is in tension with his public persona. This description stops short, however, of explaining how S accomplishes this, failing to imagine the author's literary sophistication and his background. I find the personalizing of David to be explained by S's transformation of aboriginal space into personality—in the same way that aboriginal poetry is transformed into the psalms. The group consciousness of aboriginal culture is thus made personal. Yet while Brueggemann listens to the nuances of David's words, he disappoints us by ignoring S's ear. A poet like S exists among peers, one of whom was J, and the words he gives to David's life resonate in a specific culture that scholars fear to imagine. Just as bad translations are common today, they no doubt were even more so in S's culture, which had to translate everything anew from cuneiform writing into the early Hebrew alphabet. Keeping that in mind, it is easier to understand S's playful irony toward the way royal chronicles of the past are woodenly translated.

We might call S's narrative a transformation of a typical royal chronicle for a knowing audience, bestowing an ironic sense of character as destiny and reflecting the individuality of the culture itself. Unable to imagine the irony, Brueggemann gets tangled up in theories of "substantive ambiguity" and Gerhard von Rad's "emancipated spirituality" to explain what is simply an impressive display of the writer's individuality at play. We might say the same for the great cave artists of 30,000 years ago without resorting to such lamentable terms. They played with their resources—and the responses were no doubt awe and delight.

Because he has forbidden himself to imagine a playful imagination, Brueggemann, like most scholars, resorts to quoting literary critics like Paul Ricoeur, who go to painstaking extremes to differentiate genres. Is S's genre a novel, a biography, a history, or what? In truth, S was a genre-bender, like most great writers of independent mind. Brueggemann defines him as "distinctly counter-culture" and "subversive"—but wouldn't we say the same for most great minds of the past? Let's begin, then, by reimagining the culture of S's time.

According to Weinfeld in his early masterpiece *Deuteronomy and the Deuteronomic School* (1972), the history of Israel after S was written by those who "had at their command a vast reservoir of literary material, who had developed and were capable of developing a literary technique of their own—those experienced in literary composition, and skilled with the pen and the book." These words would be apt for J and S at an earlier date but would require, in addition, the mention of these writers' skills in translating from cognate languages in cuneiform and pictogram. These scholarly skills were learned not in priestly halls but at court in the palace archives and in visits to nearby court libraries—in Ashkelon and Tyre, and perhaps as far away as Egypt and Assyria. In David's palace library, built long before the Temple was begun, the tutors would have been courtiers of the previous generation.

The use of writing to promote popular education and for other didactic purposes is described in the Book of Deuteronomy for the first time. The early sources from Solomonic times also mention writing, but in an archival role, and Weinfeld emphasizes this. A fundamental reason scholars fail to imagine the Solomonic writers—that the text itself doesn't speak more of them—elicits no questions such as "Why not?" Isn't it almost too obvious that the Deuteronomic writers, who heavily edited and rewrote so many other texts, removed descriptions of writing and reading that smacked of anything more than a didactic purpose— just as they condemned Solomon's cosmopolitanism?

We learn from the later Deuteronomic writers in the books of Kings that the altars Solomon built for his foreign wives were destroyed over three hundred years later. Meanwhile, they had existed in use "and no king-reformer had ever touched them." So only after three centuries had passed did biblical writers think to criticize Solomon's culture, even calling his trade in horses with Egypt too broad. Implicitly criticized were his love and patronage of art, gardens, and, no doubt, foreign literature. The Deuteronomic author in the Book of Joshua wrote for the first time, many centuries after the event, of Israel's "extermination" of the Canaanites. "Whereas according to older sources," Weinfeld points out, "it is quite clear that even after Joshua's death the Canaanites were still dwelling among the tribes of Israel."

The youth of David, his trouble with Saul, his romances and battles, and his life on the run are missing in S. It's hard to imagine that S did not write these episodes, since his image of David is filled with indigenous spirit and it would be natural to presume his mother was also aboriginal. This may have provided the reason for later authorities to replace S's work with other accounts of the early David. Still, it is terribly curious for so documented a life that David is never given a mother. Even in the other accounts, David retains many indigenous traits: He is a poet and musician; he is imbued with the spirit of the land; he survives by his intelligence, wit, courage, and probity.

What would David have learned from an indigenous mother that sets him apart from his brothers? He is a poet and musician—and a poet of uncanny action and speech. The power of his later psalms suggest a similar native strength and openness, traits nourished in childhood by a mother's lullabies.

I I

The

BOOK

of

DAVID

A New Translation

1

I s no one left from Saul's family—" David began, "one to accept my lovingkindness, in Jonathan's name?"

An attendant remained from Saul's retinue, one Tziva. "Your servant am I," he said, after he was called to David and the king asked, "Are you that Tziva?" The king continued: "Is anyone left from Saul's family, to whom I may grant lovingkindness, in God's name?"

"Jonathan has a son left," said Tziva to the king, "one whose feet are lame."

"Can you tell me where he is?" the king inquired. "It is nothing," Tziva responded. "In the camp of Machir, son of Ammiel, in Lo-devar." It was nothing for David to send for him. Out of Machir's settlement, who was the son of Ammiel, he appeared before the king, out of Lo-devar.

Mephibosheth, son of Jonathan—grandson of Saul—arriving in fearful submission, touched the ground with his face. "Mephibosheth," David said. "Your servant," he answered, "nothing more."

"Fear not," David continued. "In Jonathan's name, your father, I am devoted to you, in lovingkindness. The fields of your grandfather, Saul—I grant you everything. From now on, you will break your bread at my table."

He fell prostrate. "Your servant asks what service can a dead dog merit—one such as I?"

But the king affirmed to Tziva, Saul's attendant: "Everything that belonged to Saul and his line I grant to your master's son. You, your sons, your attendants—all of you will work the land for him, bring in his bread and set the table before him. Yet your master's son, Mephibosheth, will break his bread in my house."

Fifteen sons and twenty attendants—these were Tziva's. "Everything my king and master sets before his servant," said Tziva to the king, "your attendant will fulfill."

"And before Mephibosheth," said the king, "is my own table, where he eats as a king's son."

Mephibosheth had a little son, Mica, and all who lived with the family of Tziva served Mephibosheth's line. In Jerusalem it was that Mephibosheth himself lived, since he ate at the king's table from then on. He was one whose feet were lame.

❧ 2 SAMUEL 9:1–13

2

After all this, Ammon's king died, and ruling in his turn was Hanun, his son.

"Now I will grant lovingkindness to Hanun, son of Nachash," said David, "since his father's devotion was granted to me." David's hand was extended to him in consolation by his attendants, on behalf of his father. These servants of David proceeded to the land of the Ammonites.

But Ammonite leaders had advised Hanun, their ruler. "Will you believe David loves your father," they asked, "and sends friends? Are these servants of David not here instead to penetrate, explore, and expose the town?"

Hanun seized David's servants, shaved off half their beards, cut off half their battle dress—their buttocks exposed to the air—and booted them out.

When David got wind of this, he sent comfort to the men—they were humiliated. "Stay in Jericho while your beards grow back. Come back yourselves."

The Ammonites soon understood the stink before David was theirs, and they sent contracts to the Aramaeans in Beth-rehob and the Aramaeans in Zoba for twenty thousand foot soldiers, as well as a thousand more from King Maacah and twelve thousand men from Ishtob.

When David got word of this, he sent out Joab and all the veteran military.

The Ammonites marched out of their town gate and opened a front right there, while the Aramaeans of Zoba, Rehob, Ishtob, and Maacah were organized by themselves in the field.

Joab could see himself exposed from behind if he met the front, so he chose the pick of all Israel's men and assembled them against the Aramaeans. The remaining troops he put under the hand of Abishai, his brother, to array opposite the Ammonites.

"If the Aramaeans are too strong for me," he said, "you will come back to help."

"If the Ammonites are too strong for you, I will come to back you up. Be bold and boundless in the eyes of our people and beyond the cities of God, and Yahweh can do as he pleases."

Joab and all his men advanced into position for battle, and the Aramaeans fled before his eyes. The Ammonites saw it—the Aramaeans fleeing—and fell back before Abishai, into their city. Joab returned to Jerusalem, the Ammonites overcome.

The Aramaeans then understood they were outdone in the eyes of Israel, and they pulled themselves together.

Hadadezer contacts the Aramaeans who are on the other side of the river and orders them to come to Helam. Shobach, captain of Hadadezer's army, was at its head.

As David hears of this, he gathers all of Israel's men, heads across the Jordan, and also comes to Helam. The Aramaeans fall back into position against him, and battle David.

Before Israel's eyes the Aramaeans turned to flee, but the men of seven hundred Aramaean chariots were cut off by David, along with forty thousand horsemen; Shobach, their head, was cut down there.

All the kings in service to Hadadezer beheld their downfall. They turned to peace, turned into servants of Israel. The Aramaeans turned away from the extended hand of the Ammonites after this.

<p> 2 SAMUEL 10:1–19

3

Here we are: a year was passing, and it is the season best for the wars of kings. David sends out Joab, his own retinue, and all of Israel's army, and they bring the Ammonites to their knees, besieging Rabbah. Meanwhile, David lingered in Jerusalem.

It happens one late afternoon that David rises from his bed, takes a walk around the palace roof, and from there, his glance falls upon a woman in her bath. The woman appeared very beautiful in his eyes.

David sent messengers to uncover more about the woman. "Of course, that must be Bathsheba," someone said, "the daughter of Eliam and wife of Uriah, the Hittite."

Now David sent his assistants—they besieged her—and she enters before his eyes. He lay with her in his bed, since her period had passed and she was purified, and then she returned to her house.

The woman conceived and sent word—"I am pregnant," she revealed to David.

Now word from David reaches Joab—"Have Uriah the Hittite sent to me"—and Joab conveyed Uriah to David.

David questions Uriah when he enters, wanting to know how Joab fared, how the forces were doing, how the war was going.

"Go home and bathe your feet," David directed Uriah, and as he went out of the king's palace a spread of meats from the king was sent down to him.

But Uriah bedded down at the palace gate, in the quarters of his king's courtiers, and did not descend to his own house.

David was told—"Uriah did not proceed to his house"—and confronted him with these words: "Haven't you come from the road? Why didn't you return to your house?"

"The ark rests in a tent," Uriah said to David. "Israel, Judah—they are encamped; my commander, Joab, and your own regiment camp in the open. Do I just go into my own house, eat and drink, and sleep with my wife? On your life—and as flesh breathes—I cannot do that."

"Then rest today as well," said David, "and tomorrow you will go out." So Uriah lodged in Jerusalem the rest of the day and next, when David had him summoned to eat and drink in the king's presence until he was made intoxicated. Yet in the evening, instead of going home, Uriah returns to bed down among Israel's courtiers.

Here we are: in the morning, David composes a letter for Joab, sending it by Uriah's hand. "Move Uriah into the spear-head of the fighting," his letter read, "and then fall back until he's laid bare to his death."

So it happens: Joab explores his siege of the city and moves Uriah into a probing unit of fighters. The defenders of the city thrust out and attack Joab, and some of the lives of David's servants are lost, Uriah the Hittite fallen among the dead.

Presently Joab conveyed to David a thorough account of the fighting, directing the messenger to say: "When you finish telling the king everything about the war, the king may be furious and ask, 'Why did you approach so close to the city when you struck—too dumb to remember they could shoot from the wall? So who killed Abimelech, son of Jerubbesheth—if it wasn't a woman dropping a piece of millstone on him from the wall at The-bez, blotting him out? Why advance so close to the wall?' Now you will add: 'Your servant, Uriah the Hittite, is among the dead.'"

Out the messenger went, arriving before David and announcing precisely what Joab had directed. "It seemed their men were succeeding against us," recounted the messenger to David, "coming out to attack us in the open, but we pushed them back to their gate. Their archers then shot at your men from the wall, and some of the king's servants fell. Your servant Uriah the Hittite is among the dead."

Said David to the messenger, "Tell Joab this: 'Do not become disturbed about it. The sword cuts down one as well as another.

Strengthen your attack on the city, penetrate it.' And offer him comfort."

As Uriah's wife comprehends the words telling of her husband Uriah's death, she wails for her husband. The period of mourning passes, and David conveys his wishes: he has her conveyed to his palace, where she becomes his wife and bears him a son.

It was a disloyal thing David had done before the eyes of Yahweh.

❧ 2 SAMUEL 11:1–27

4

Now Yahweh sent Nathan to David. Nathan went to him, to tell: "Two men were in the same city, one rich, the other, poor. The rich man had a legion of sheep and cattle; the poor man had nothing but a little ewe lamb that he had bought. He cared for her, and it grew up together with him and his children. It shared his own morsels of food, drank from his cup, and snuggled in his lap; it was like a daughter to him.

"It happened a traveller visited the rich man, but when it came to making a meal for this visitor stopping with him, he spared his own flocks and herds and took instead the poor man's lamb. And then he fixed it for the man who had come to him."

David's face was ablaze with fury against the man. "As Yahweh lives, the life of the man who did that will not be spared," said David to Nathan. "He will replace the lamb four times over, because he spared no gesture of kindness in this deed."

But Nathan said to David, "You are that man. Here is what Yahweh, the God of Israel, says: 'I anointed you king over Israel, I released you from Saul's grasp. I gave you your master's house, your master's wives fell in your lap. I gave you the House of Israel and Judah, and if that is not enough, I would double and quadruple it. Why then have you defied Yahweh's desire—disloyal before his eyes? You have dispatched Uriah the Hittite with sword, turned his wife into your wife, cut him down by the blade of the Ammonites.

"'So be it: the sword will never depart from your house, because you have been disloyal to me, grasped the hand of the wife of Uriah the Hittite to be your wife.'

"So says Yahweh: 'Look well: I will uncover disloyalty for you in your own house. I will deliver your wives, before your very eyes, to your neighbor, and he will lay with them under this very sun. Since you did this in secret, I will make it happen before the eyes of all Israel. It will be broad daylight.'"

David said, "I have betrayed Yahweh." And Nathan answered David, "Yahweh has dispatched your disloyalty away from himself; you will not die. Still, your deed bears out contempt before Yahweh's enemies; the child born to you will have to die."

As Nathan walked back home, it turns out Yahweh encounters David's child, born of Uriah's wife; it is deathly ill.

David besieges God for the child: he fasted, hid himself, lay all night on the ground. The senior advisers in the palace stood over him and tried to coax him up but he could not bear them now, nor would he eat with them.

Look: seven days pass and the child is dead. But David's attendants are panicked to tell him the child has died; and among each other, they say, "He couldn't bear us when we spoke while the child was alive—what terror will grip him when we tell him the child is dead?"

Noticing that his servants are whispering, David understands that the child is dead. "Is the child dead?" he asks. "Departed," they say.

David rises from the ground, bathes and oils himself, changes into fresh clothes, and goes to the House of Yahweh, prostrating himself. He returns to his own house, requests food; they set it before him, and so he eats.

"Why do you bear yourself in this way?" asked his courtiers. "You fasted and wept for the child when he was sick, and now when he is dead, you go out and eat a meal."

He replied, "I fasted and wept while the child was still alive, because I thought, 'How can one know if God will spare some kindness for me, and allow the child to live?' Now that he is dead, what is the use of fasting? Can I bring him back again? I may go to him, but he can never come back to me."

David consoles Bathsheba, his wife; he goes to her and lays with her; she bears a son whom she named Solomon; and Yahweh loves him, sending a name by the prophet Nathan's hand: Jedidiah he calls him, beloved of Yahweh.

Meanwhile, Joab had struck the Ammonite city of Rabbah,

imperiling the royal grounds. Messengers from Joab arrived before David, saying: "I have struck Rabbah and captured their water-supply. Assemble the rest of the army, besiege the city and capture it, or else my name will be linked to it, if I take it myself."

David summons the rest of the army, besieges the city and takes it. Then he takes the gold crown from the head of the royal idol, weighing about a hundred pounds, and from it the jewel—to be fitted on the head of David. He also bears off a massive amount of spoils from the city.

The citizens within were conveyed out, and he put them under the rule of saws and sledges and iron axes, or settled them into brickmaking. All Ammonite cities were treated equally, until David and the army could depart for Jerusalem.

❧ 2 SAMUEL 12:1–31

5

Much has happened, but now look closely: it becomes clear that Absalom, David's son, has a beautiful sister, Tamar her name, and a son of David, Amnon, loves her. But Amnon is sick with a mess of feelings for his sister Tamar—she is a virgin, besides—and it is a forbidding task to imagine what to do with her.

However, Amnon had a friend in Jonadab, the son of David's brother Shimah, and Jonadab was quite an intelligent man. "You are a prince," he told him, "so why are you just dragging yourself through these days? Can't you tell me?"

"I love Tamar, the sister of Absalom, my brother," Amnon told him.

Now Jonadab says, "Lie in your bed and make believe you are sick, and when your father comes to see you, say to him, 'Allow my sister Tamar to come and make my supper. Permit her to fix a meal in my presence, so I can see what it is, and grant that she serve me with her own hands.'"

Amnon lay down and made himself sick. The king came to see him, and Amnon pleaded, "Please, allow my sister Tamar to come and fix some cakes before my eyes, and permit her to feed them to me."

David sent word for Tamar at home: "Go to your brother Amnon's house, and make him a meal." Tamar goes to the house of her brother Amnon, while he is lying in bed; then, she prepares dough and kneads it into cakes while he watches, and she bakes the cakes. She finds a pan and serves them, but he turns down the food.

"Let the men all leave," Amnon says, and the servants depart.

"Bring the food to my room, so you can feed me," Amnon implores Tamar. But as she brings them into the room to eat, he embraces her: "Come lie with me, sister," he says.

"No, my brother, do not rape me," she said, "these things are not done in Israel. Do not embrace contempt. Where would I go with such a smear? And you, you will become a joke in Israel. Please, speak to the king, and he will not turn you away from me." But he will not listen to her; stronger than she, he pushes her down and lies with her.

Afterward, Amnon felt a great disgust with her; now his dislike of her was greater than the love he had borne. "Get dressed and leave," Amnon said to her.

"No, not now," she replied, "to send me away is a coarser thing than the first contempt you held me in." But he would not listen to her.

He called his personal servant, and said, "Take this woman out of my sight, and lock the door behind her." She is wearing a many-colored gown, the customary clothes for princesses who are still virgins—as the servant takes her outside and bars the door behind her.

But Tamar puts dirt on her head, and rips the gown of many colors she is dressed in; and she tears at her hair, and goes away screaming.

"Was your brother Amnon the one who did this?" asked Absalom, her brother. "For now, sister, be silent about it; he is your brother. Do not dwell on it." Tamar stayed in her brother Absalom's house, but she was crushed.

Word came to King David of all these things, and he was furious. Absalom would not speak to his brother Amnon, neither a good word nor bad, yet Absalom was disgusted with Amnon for raping his sister Tamar.

What happens now—a full two years later, when Absalom is having a sheepshearing in Baalhazor, which is next to

Ephraim—is that he invites all the king's sons. Absalom goes to the king and says, "Your servant is making a major sheepshearing. If it pleases you, will the king and his courtiers accompany your servant?"

"No, my son, we should not all go," the king said to Absalom. "It is too burdensome for you." Absalom urged him to go, but he would not, bidding him farewell.

"If not," said Absalom, "please allow my brother Amnon to accompany us."

The king replied, "Let him not go with you." But Absalom persisted, and he let Amnon and all the princes go with him.

Absalom gave these instructions to his men: "Pay attention to Amnon, and when the wine goes to his head and I say strike, then kill him. Show no fear and remember: haven't I ordered you? Be strong and act with confidence."

Absalom's servants do to Amnon as Absalom instructed, alarming all the other princes, who climb on their mules and flee.

Now it happens they are still on the road when this news reaches David: Absalom has killed all the king's sons and not one survives.

Alarmed, the king rises and rips apart his clothes and lies on the ground, with all his attendants standing over him in their torn coats. But Jonadab, the son of David's brother Shimah, declares: "My master must not believe all the young princes are dispatched. Amnon alone is dead, as was Absalom's intention ever since he raped his sister Tamar. So the king my master cannot believe for an instant that all the king's sons are dead, when only Amnon is departed."

Meanwhile, Absalom had departed with his life.

Now the sentinel spots a large group as it suddenly appears coming around the back side of the hill opposite. "Look, the princes," says Jonadab to the king. "As I am your attendant, my words accompany the men." It happens, when he has hardly finished speaking, that the princes arrive and burst into tears, and the king broke out sobbing, as did all his retinue, uncontrollably.

But Absalom had fled, gone to Talmai, King Ammihud of Geshur's son. Yet David grieved for his son day after day. Absalom remained in Geshur three years. King David's heart ached to see Absalom but he was consoled by now for Amnon; what was the use, seeing he was dead.

🌱 2 SAMUEL 13:1–39

6

When Joab son of Zeruiah noticed that the king's heart would not bend from Absalom, he sent word to Tekoah and hired a wise woman, and instructed her: "Act like a mourner and dress in mourning clothes and without makeup; play a woman who has grieved long days for someone vanished. Go to the king and perform this part for him." Now Joab puts the words in her mouth.

The woman of Tekoah speaks to the king, but first prostrates herself, and calls out—her face to the ground—"Save me, Your Majesty."

"What's wrong with you?" the king asks.

"I am a widow, my husband is dead," she begins. "Your humble housemaid had two sons, who began to fight out in the field, and there was no one around to stop them, until one of them knocked the other down, killing him. And now the whole family has turned against your humble housemaid, and they cry, 'Turn over the one who struck down his brother, so we may take his life for taking a brother's, even if we have to extinguish the heir as well.' That is how they would extinguish the last coal left burning on my hearth, and leave my husband without name or vestige on the face of the earth."

"Go home," said the king to the woman. "I will rule on your behalf."

"Your Majesty the king," said the woman of Tekoah to the king, "let the stain be mine and on my father's line; let the king and his throne remain clean."

The king replied, "Let anyone say another thing to you—I will have him brought here, and he will not touch you again."

"Let Your Majesty remember Yahweh, your God," she said, "and hold back the unbound hands of revenge, before they smash my son."

The king replied, "On Yahweh's life, not one hair of your son's will touch the ground."

"Let your humble housemaid say one word more to Your Majesty," the woman said. "Say it," he said.

"Why have you acted in the same way you yourself played out a similar plot against God's people?" the woman began. "In the judgment you have made for me you condemn yourself— since you turn away from your own outcast.

"No man escapes death; we are like water drained into the ground that cannot be collected again. But God will not turn from a life that can make this judgment: no man should remain an outcast.

"That is why I have come to appeal to Your Majesty, alarmed by those people. Your humble housemaid thought, 'I will speak to the king and what I ask, be granted by a king. The king may listen, and sever the grasp of those who would sever me and my son from their God-given inheritance.'

"Finally, your humble housemaid said to herself, 'The word of His Majesty may bring peace. He sees right from wrong like God's own angel.' May Yahweh, your God, be with you."

Now the king says to the woman, "Do not withhold from me what I may ask." And the woman answers, "Speak, Your Majesty."

"Is Joab behind you in any of this?" asks the king.

"As sure as you live, Your Majesty, I cannot turn from what you say," she says. "True, your servant Joab directed me, putting all these words in the mouth of your housemaid. To shape the true purpose of these words, your servant Joab withheld his role. But Your Majesty is wise as an angel who can see through all earthly things."

Turning to Joab, the king says, "It is done. Depart, and return my boy Absalom again."

Joab kneels to the ground, then prostrates himself, thanking the king. "This day," says Joab, "your servant knows he has your faith. The king has performed his servant's purpose."

Now Joab proceeds and arrives in Geshur, bringing Absalom to Jerusalem. "To his own house take him," said the king, "and to my face may he not be taken." So Absalom returned to his house, and did not see the king's face. Yet throughout Israel there was none to be admired as Absalom was, for his beauty. It was said that from the sole of his foot to the hair on his head there was no defect in him. And when he cut his hair, which he had to do every year, as it grew too heavy, the fallen hair weighed two hundred shekels by the royal weight.

Absalom had three sons, and a daughter whose name was also Tamar, and she too was a beauty. He lived in Jerusalem two years without appearing before the king. Then Absalom sent for Joab, who could arrange for him to be presented to the king, but Joab would not come to him. He sent for him again, and again he would not come. He turned to his servants: "You know that Joab's field is next to mine, and he plants barley there. Go and set it on fire." Absalom's servants set the field on fire.

Now Joab comes right away to Absalom's house, saying to him, "Why have your servants set fire to my field?"

"I sent for you to come here," Absalom replies. "I want to send you to the king to present my words: 'Why did I leave Geshur? I would be better off if I were still there. Now I would be taken to the king, and if there is some defect in me, why then, take my life.'"

Joab goes to the king, presents all this, and in response, Absalom is summoned. He comes to the king and throws himself facedown to the ground before him. The king kissed Absalom.

❦   2 SAMUEL 14:1–33

7

Sometime afterward, Absalom provided himself with a chariot, horses, and fifty men to run before him. He took to rising early and stationing himself by the road to the city gates, so when a man had a case that was pending before the king, Absalom called out to him, "What city are you from?" When he heard, "Your servant is from one of the tribes in Israel," Absalom said, "I am sure that your claim is fair and just, but no one is assigned to you by the king to hear it. If I were made judge in the land," Absalom went on, "everyone with a legal dispute that came before me would be sure to get fair justice."

Further, if a man approached who bowed to him, Absalom extended his hand, took hold of him, and kissed him. He did this to every Israelite who came to the king for judgment. With this practice, Absalom won the hearts of the men of Israel.

Here we are: four years have gone by. "Allow me to go to Hebron and perform the vow to Yahweh I have made," Absalom said to the king. "Your servant vowed these words when I lived in Geshur of Aram: 'If Yahweh takes me back to Jerusalem, I will serve him.'" The king answered "Go in peace." He set out for Hebron.

But Absalom sent his attendants to all the tribes of Israel to say, "When you hear the sound of the horn, announce that Absalom has become king in Hebron." Meanwhile, two hundred men left Jerusalem with Absalom. Having been invited, they went in good faith, suspecting nothing. Absalom also asked Ahithophel the Gilonite, David's counselor, to come from Gilo and be present as the promised sacrifices were fulfilled. The conspiracy gained strength, as the numbers swelled at Absalom's side.

One of them, however, comes to David: "The hearts of Israel are turned toward Absalom." David turns to all the courtiers with him in Jerusalem: "We must be prepared to run, or none of us will escape from Absalom. We must get out fast, or he will intercept us and we will meet with disaster, the city turned to the sword." And the king's courtiers say to a man, "Whatever my lord the king judges, your servant is prepared."

Now the king went out, followed by his entire household. But he left ten of his women, concubines, to look after the palace. As the king was going, the people following behind, he stopped at the last house.

All his followers marched past him, including Cherethites

and Pelethites and Gittites, all of them—and six hundred men who had accompanied him from Gath, also marched by the king.

The king said to Ittai the Gittite, "Why should you too go with us? Go back and stay with the new king, for you are a foreigner and you are also an exile from your country. And you arrived only yesterday. Do I make you wander around with us today, when I must run wherever I can? Go back, and take your companions with you, and lovingkindness go with you."

"As the Lord Yahweh lives and as my lord the king lives," said Ittai to the king, "wherever the king goes, whether in death or life, there your servant will be."

"Then go on by," said David to Ittai. And Ittai the Gittite and all his men and the children who were with him passed by.

The whole landscape was weeping aloud as the army passed by. The king crossed the Kidron Valley, as all the troops had crossed it, on the road to the wilderness.

Look well: Zadok was there also, and the Levites carrying the Ark of the Covenant of God, which they set down until all the people had passed out of the city. Abiathar also had appeared.

But the king said to Zadok, "Take the Ark of God back to the city. If Yahweh looks kindly on me, he will bring me back and show it to me again—and in its resting place. But if he should say, 'I do not want you,' I am ready. He can do with me as he pleases."

The king spoke again to Zadok the priest: "Are you not a seer? Return to the city in peace, with your two sons—your own son Ahimaaz and Abiathar's son, Jonathan. See well. I will stay in the protection of the wilderness until word comes from you to inform me."

Zadok and Abiathar brought the Ark of God back to Jerusalem, and they stayed on there, while David went up the slope of the Mount of Olives, weeping as he ascended, his head covered and walking barefoot. And all the people who were with him covered their heads and wept as they went up.

Now David heard: "Ahithophel is among the conspirators with Absalom." And David responded, "May it please Yahweh to turn the sagacity of Ahithophel into lunacy."

David reaches the top of mount, where people have kissed the ground before God, and now look: Hushai the Archite is there to meet him, but with his coat ripped open and earth upon his head. "If you go on with us, you become our burden," David says to him. "But if you go back to the city and say to Absalom, 'I will be your servant, O king. I was your father's servant in the past—as I will now be yours,' then, on my behalf, you may undo the sage advice of Ahithophel.

"Besides, the priests Zadok and Abiathar will be there with you, and with everything that you hear in the king's palace you may inform Zadok and Abiathar, the priests. Listen well: their two sons are there with them, Zadok's son Ahimaaz and Abiathar's son, Jonathan, and through them you may inform me of everything you hear."

So it is: Hushai, the friend of David, reaches the city as Absalom was entering Jerusalem.

🌱 2 SAMUEL 15:1–37

8

David passes a little beyond the summit and now look: Ziba the servant of Mephibosheth is coming toward him with a pair of saddled asses, and upon them two hundred loaves of bread, one hundred cakes of raisin, one hundred cakes of summer figs, and jar of wine.

"What are you doing with these?" the king asked Ziba. "The asses are for Your Majesty's family to ride on," Ziba answered, "and the bread and figs are for your attendants to eat, and the wine is to drink by those who are exhausted in the wilderness."

"And where is your master's son?" the king continued. "He is staying in Jerusalem," Ziba told the king. "He said to us: 'Tomorrow, the House of Israel will give me back the throne of my grandfather.'"

"Then all that belongs to Mephibosheth will now be yours," the king said to Ziba. And Ziba replied, "My lord, may it please Your Majesty that I deserve such graciousness, a minion such as I."

King David approaches Bahurim, and now look: a member comes toward him of Saul's family. His name: Shimei son of Gera, and he is hurling curses as he comes. He throws stones at David and all King David's courtiers, while all the people and all the warriors stand at his right and his left.

"Get out, get out, you beast, you outcast," are among the curses that flew. "Yahweh is paying you back for all your crimes against the family of Saul, after you took his place. Yahweh is delivering your throne to your son Absalom, and you are on the run because you are an outlaw."

Abishai son of Zeruiah said to the king, "Why let that dead dog abuse my lord the king? Let me go over and take off his head."

"What has this to do with you, you sons of Zeruiah?" the king stepped in. "He is abusive only because Yahweh told him to curse David, so who is to say, 'Why did you do that?'"

David turned to Abishai and all the courtiers: "If my son, out of my own loins, is hoping to kill me, how much more this Benjaminite. Let him go on with his curses, since Yahweh has told him to. It may happen that Yahweh will look upon me kindly in my punishment and reward me for the curses spoken today."

So David and his men continued on their way, while Shimei walked alongside on the slope of the hill, cursing him as he walked, and throwing stones at him and flinging dirt.

The king and all who were accompanying him arrived exhausted. They rested there. Meanwhile, Absalom and all the people, the men of Israel, arrived in Jerusalem, together with Ahithophel.

When Hushai the Archite, David's friend, appeared before Absalom, Hushai said to him, "Long live the king. Long live the king."

But Absalom said, "Is this your kindness to your friend? Why didn't you go with your friend?"

"No," Hushai replied. "I am for the one whom Yahweh and

this people and all the men of Israel have chosen, and I will stay with him. Besides, whom should I serve, if not David's son? I was your father's servant in the past—as I will now be yours."

Absalom turned to Ahithophel, "What would you advise us to do?"

"Have intercourse with your father's concubines," Ahithophel advised him, "these whom he left to mind the palace. When all Israel hears that you have challenged the anger of your father, all who support you will be strengthened in resolve."

So they pitched a tent for Absalom on the roof, and Absalom lay with his father's concubines before the eyes of all Israel.

In those days, a man accepted the advice Ahithophel gave as if he had asked an oracle of God. That is how the advice of Ahithophel was respected, both by David and by Absalom.

❧ 2 SAMUEL 16:1-23

9

"Let me pick twelve thousand men and I will proceed tonight in pursuit of David," Ahithophel was now saying to Absalom. "I will come upon him when he is sad and exhausted, and I will put him into a panic. As all the forces with him run away, I will kill the king alone.

"In this way I will bring all his people back to you. When they have all come back—except the man you are after—all the people will be at peace."

The advice was pleasing to Absalom and all the elders of Israel.

"Summon Hushai the Archite as well," Absalom was saying, "so we can hear what he too has to say."

When Hushai appeared before Absalom, he heard: "This is what Ahithophel has advised. Shall we follow his advice? If not, what do you say?"

"This time the advice that Ahithophel has given is not good," Hushai said to Absalom. "You know that your father and his men are brave fighters," Hushai continued, "and they will be as desperate as a bear in the wild robbed of her cubs. Your father is too experienced a soldier to sleep among his men.

"Open your eyes and you will see that even now he must be hiding in one of the pits or in some other place. And if any of our men fall in the first attack, whoever hears of it will say, 'The forces that follow Absalom are being slaughtered.' Even if he is a brave man with the heart of a lion, he will be shaken—for all Israel knows that your father and the soldiers with him are ferocious fighters.

"Thus I advise that all Israel from Dan to Beersheba, that number as the sands of the sea, be called up to join you, and that you yourself march into battle. When we find him in whatever place he may be, we will fall upon him as the dew falling on the ground. No one will survive, neither he nor any of the men with him.

"And if he retreats into a city, all Israel will bring ropes to that city and drag its stones as far as the riverbed, until not even a pebble of it is left."

Absalom and all Israel agreed that the advice of Hushai the Archite was better than that of Ahithophel.

"Such and such is what Ahithophel advised Absalom and the elders of Israel," Hushai told Zadok and Abiathar, the priests, "and such and such is what I advised. Now send this message right away to David: 'Do not spend the night at the fords of the wilderness, but pass over at once, or else the king and all his forces will be overwhelmed and sunk.'"

Jonathan and Ahimaaz were staying at En-rogel, not wanting to risk being seen entering the city, and an outcast girl would go out to bring them word, and they would then go and acquaint King David. Yet a boy saw them and acquainted Absalom, so they left right away and came to the house of a man in Bahurim who had a well in his courtyard. They got down into it, as the wife found a cloth, spread it over the mouth of the well, and scattered groats on top of it, so that nothing would be noticed.

Absalom's servants came to the woman at the house, asking, "Where are Ahimaaz and Jonathan?" The woman said that they had crossed a bit beyond the water. They searched, but found nothing before they returned to Jerusalem.

Now look: they are gone, and the two come up from the well and go to inform King David. "Be prepared to cross the water quickly," they said to David, "for Ahithophel has advised such and such concerning you."

David and all the people with him pass over the Jordan, and by daybreak not one is left who has not reached the other side.

When Ahithophel saw that his advice had not been followed, he saddled his ass and went back to his hometown, where he ordered his affairs and then hanged himself. He was buried in his ancestral tomb.

David had already reached Mahanaim when Absalom and all the men of Israel with him crossed the Jordan.

Absalom had made Amasa army commander in place of Joab. Amasa was the son of a man named Ithra the Israelite, who had lain with Abigail, daughter of Nahash and sister of Joab's mother Zeruiah. Now the Israelites and Absalom made camp in the district of Gilead.

So it happens: David reaches Mahanaim, and Shobi son of Nahash from Rabbath-ammon, Machir son of Ammiel from Lodevar, and Barzillai the Gileadite from Rogelim present couches, basins, and earthenware, along with wheat, barley, flour, parched grain, beans, lentils, honey, curds, a flock, and cheese from the herd for David and the people with him to eat. "The people must surely have grown hungry, and exhausted, and thirsty in the wilderness," they say.

❦ 2 SAMUEL 17:1–29

1 0

David assembled the soldiers who were with him, naming captains for troops of thousands, and captains of hundreds. Out went the troops, one-third under the command of Joab, one-third under the command of Joab's brother Abishai son of Zeruiah, and a third under the command of Ittai the Gittite. "I myself will march out with you," David said to the troops.

"No!" they said. "For if some of us flee, the rest will not be concerned about us; even if half of us should die, the others will not be concerned about us. But you are worth ten thousand of us. Therefore, it is better for you to support us from the town."

The king said to them, "I will do whatever you think best."

So the king stood beside the gate as all the soldiers marched out by the hundreds and thousands. The king gave orders to Joab, Abishai, and Ittai: "Deal gently with my boy Absalom, for my sake." All the troops heard the king give the order about Absalom to all the officers.

The soldiers trooped out into the open to confront the Israelites, and the battle was fought in the forest of Ephraim. The Israelite army was routed by David's followers, and a great slaughter took place there that day—twenty thousand men.

The battle spread out over that whole region, and the forest seemed to devour more soldiers that day than the sword.

Absalom encountered some of David's followers as he was riding on a mule, and as the mule passed under the tangled branches of a great terebinth, his hair got caught in the tree: he was suspended between heaven and earth but the mule under him kept going.

One of the men saw it and told Joab, "I have just seen Absalom hanging from a terebinth."

"You saw it!" Joab said to the man who told him. "Why didn't you kill him then and there? I would have owed you ten shekels of silver and a belt."

But the man answered Joab, "Even if I had a thousand shekels of silver in my hands, I would not raise a hand against the king's son. The king directed you, Abishai, and Ittai in our presence: 'Let no one touch my boy Absalom, for my sake.' If I betrayed myself—and nothing is hidden from the king—you would have stood aloof."

"Then I will not wait for you," said Joab. He took three darts in his hand and drove them into Absalom's chest. He was still alive in the thick growth of the terebinth, when ten of Joab's young arms-bearers closed in and struck at Absalom until he died.

Then Joab sounded the shofar, and the army halted their pursuit of the Israelites; Joab kept rein on the soldiers. They took Absalom and flung him into a large pit in the forest, and they piled up a huge heap of stones over it. Meanwhile, all the Israelites fled to their homes.

Keep in mind that while he was alive, Absalom had taken the pillar which is in the Valley of the King and set it up for himself, explaining, "I have no son to keep my name alive." He had named the pillar after himself, and it has been called Absalom's Monument to this day.

"Let me run and report," said Ahimaaz, son of Zadok, "that the Lord has avenged the king against his enemies."

But Joab said to him, "You will not be the one with the news today. You may bring news some other day, but you'll not bring any today—the king's son is dead." And Joab turned to an African: "Go tell the king what you have seen." The African bowed to Joab and ran off.

Ahimaaz, son of Zadok, insisted, "No matter what, let me run, too, behind the African." Joab asked, "Why run, my boy, when you have no news worth telling?" "I am going to run anyway." "Then run," he said. So Ahimaaz ran by way of the plain, and he passed the African.

David was sitting between the two gates. The watchman on the roof of the gate walked over to the city wall, and in the distance he saw a man running alone. The watchman called down and told the king; and the king said, "If he is alone, he has news to report." As he was coming nearer, the watchman saw another man running, and he called out to the gatekeeper, "There is another man running alone." And the king said, "That one, too, brings news."

"I can see that the first one runs like Ahimaaz son of Zadok," said the watchman. The king answered: "He is a good man, and he comes with good news."

Ahimaaz called out and said to the king, "All is well." He kneeled, face to the ground, and said, "Praises to Yahweh, your God, who exposed to us the men who raised their hand against Your Majesty, the king."

The king asked, "Is my boy Absalom safe?" And Ahimaaz answered, "I saw a large crowd when Your Majesty's servant Joab was sending your humble servant off, but I don't know what it was about."

"Step aside and stand over there," said the king. He stepped aside and waited. Just then the African arrived, saying: "Let Your Majesty the king be informed that Yahweh has avenged you today against all who rebelled against you."

"Is my boy Absalom safe?" the king asked the African. The African replied, "May the enemies of Your Majesty the king and all who rose against you to do you harm turn out like that young man!"

The king shook. He mounted to the upper chamber of the gateway and wept, moaning these words as he went, "My son Absalom! O my son, my son Absalom! If only I had died instead of you! O Absalom, my son, my son!"

❧ 2 SAMUEL 18:1-33

11

Mark well: After Joab is told that the king is weeping and mourning over Absalom, the victory day turns into one of

mourning for the whole army, as they hear that very day that
the king grieves for his son. They steal into town that day like
an army in shame, after running away in battle.

The king covers his face and keeps crying aloud, "O my son
Absalom! O Absalom, my son, my son!" Joab comes to the king
in his quarters, saying, "Today you have shamed the faces of all
your followers, who this day saved your life, and the lives of
your sons and daughters, and the lives of your wives and concubines, by showing love for those who hate you and hate for
those who love you. You have made clear today that the officers
and men mean nothing to you. I am sure that if Absalom were
alive today and the rest of us dead, you would have preferred it.

"Now get yourself together, come out and placate your followers. I swear by Yahweh that if you do not come out, not a
single man will remain with you overnight. That would be a
greater disaster for you than any disaster that has struck you
from your youth until now."

The king prepares himself, sits down in the gateway, and
when the warriors are told that the king is sitting there, they all
present themselves to the king.

Meanwhile the Israelites flee to their homes. All the people
throughout the tribes of Israel were arguing: Some say, "The
king saved us from the hands of our enemies, and he delivered
us from the hands of the Philistines, and just now he had to
escape the country because of Absalom. But Absalom, whom we
anointed over us, has died in battle; why then do you sit idle
instead of escorting the king back?"

The talk of all Israel reaches the king in his quarters. So King
David sends this message to the priests Zadok and Abiathar:

"Speak to the elders of Judah and say, 'Why should you be the last to bring the king back to his palace? You are my family, as my own flesh and blood. Why should you be the last to escort the king back?'

"And to Amasa say this, 'You are my own flesh and blood. May God do such and more to me if you do not become my army commander once and for all, in place of Joab.'"

Amasa changes the hearts of all the Judahites as one man. They send a message to the king: "Come back with all your followers."

The king started back, arriving at the Jordan as the Judahites come to Gilgal to meet the king and to bring him across the Jordan. Shimei son of Gera, the Benjaminite from Bahurim, hurried down with the Judahites to meet King David, accompanied by a thousand Benjaminites. And Ziba, the servant of the House of Saul, together with his fifteen sons and twenty slaves, rushed down to the Jordan ahead of the king while the crossing was being made, to escort the king's family over, and to do whatever he wished.

Shimei son of Gera flung himself before the king as he was about to cross the Jordan. He said to him, "May my lord not hold me guilty, nor remember the curses your servant committed on the day my lord the king left Jerusalem. May Your Majesty give it no thought. Your servant knows that he has offended, so I have come down today, the first of all the House of Joseph, to meet my lord the king."

But Abishai son of Zeruiah interrupted, "Shouldn't Shimei be put to death for that—cursing Yahweh's anointed one?"

"What has this to do with you, you sons of Zeruiah, that you should cross me today?" said the king. "Should a single Israelite be put to death today? Don't I know that today I am again king over Israel?"

Then the king turned to Shimei: "You shall not die," on which the king gave him his oath.

Mephibosheth, the grandson of Saul, also came down to meet the king. He had not pared his toenails, or trimmed his mustache, or washed his clothes from the day that the king left until the day he returned safe. When he arrived from Jerusalem, the king asked him, "Why didn't you come with me, Mephibosheth?"

"My lord the king, my own servant deceived me. I, your servant, planned to saddle my ass and ride on it and go with Your Majesty—for your servant is lame. Ziba has slandered your servant to my lord. But the king is like an angel of Yahweh, and may you do as pleases you. All the members of my father's family deserved only death from my lord the king, yet you brought your servant to eat at your table. What right have I to appeal further to Your Majesty?"

"You need not speak further," the king said to him. "I decree that you and Ziba shall divide the property." But Mephibosheth answered, "Let him take it all, as long as my lord the king has come home safe."

Barzillai the Gileadite had come down from Rogelin and passed on to the Jordan with the king, to see him off at the Jordan. Barzillai was very old, eighty years of age, and he had provided the king with food during his stay at Mahanaim, since he was a very wealthy man. "Cross over with me," the king said to Barzillai, "and I will provide for you in Jerusalem at my side." But

Barzillai said, "How many years are left to me that I should go up with Your Majesty to Jerusalem? I am now eighty years old. Can I tell the difference between good and bad? Can your servant taste what he eats and drinks? Can I still listen to the singing of men and women? Why then should your servant continue to be a burden to my lord the king? Your servant could barely cross the Jordan. Why should Your Majesty reward me so generously? Let your servant go back, and let me die in my own town, near the graves of my father and mother. But here is your servant Chimham—let him cross with my lord the king, and do for him as pleases you."

"Chimham shall cross with me," the king said, "and I will do for him as pleases *you*—and anything you want me to do, I will do for you."

All the people crossed the Jordan. When he was ready to cross, the king kissed Barzillai farewell, who returned to his home. The king passed on to Gilgal, with Chimham accompanying him. All the Judahite forces and part of the Israelite army escorted the king across.

Then all the men of Israel came to the king, saying, "Why did our cousins, men of Judah, steal you away and escort the king and his family across the Jordan, along with all David's men?"

"Because the king is our relative," the men of Judah replied to the men of Israel. "Why should it upset you? Have we consumed anything that belongs to the king? Has he given us any gifts?"

But the men of Israel had an answer for the men of Judah: "We have ten parts in the king [ten tribes to your two], and in

David, too, we have more than you. Why then have you slighted us? Were we not the first to propose that our king be brought back?"

However, the men of Judah prevailed over the men of Israel.

❦   2 SAMUEL 19:1-43

1 2

A beast named Sheba son of Bichri, a Benjaminite, happened to be there. He blew the horn and announced:

"We have no portion in David,

No part in Jesse's son!

Every man to his tent, O Israel!"

Watch: the men of Israel leave David and follow Sheba son of Bichri, while the men of Judah accompany their king from the Jordan to Jerusalem.

David goes to his palace in Jerusalem, and he takes the ten women concubines he had left to keep the palace and puts them in a secluded place. He will feed them, but he will not have intercourse with them. They will remain shut in retirement until the day they die, in living widowhood.

"Call up the men of Judah to my order," the king says to

Amasa, "and report here three days from now." Amasa goes to call up Judah, but takes longer than the time allotted. David turns to Abishai: "This Sheba son of Bichri will bring us more trouble than Absalom. Take your lord's servants and pursue him, before he reaches a walled city and escapes us."

Joab's men, the Cherethites and Pelethites, and all the warriors, march out behind him. In pursuit of Sheba son of Bichri, they leave Jerusalem, and just near the great stone in Gibeon, Amasa appears before them. Joab is wearing his military dress, with his sword fixed over it and fastened around his waist in its sheath, and as he steps forward, it falls out.

"How are you, brother?" Joab says to Amasa, and with his right hand Joab grabs hold of Amasa's beard as if to kiss him. Amasa was not on his guard against the sword in Joab's left hand, and Joab drives it into his belly so that his entrails pour out on the ground and he dies. He does not need to strike him a second time.

Joab and his brother Abishai then go off in pursuit of Sheba son of Bichri, while one of Joab's followers stands by the corpse, announcing "Those who approve of Joab, and who are on David's side, follow Joab."

Meanwhile Amasa lays in the middle of the road, drenched in his blood, and the man sees that everyone is stopping. When he realizes that all the people are going to stand stark still, he drags Amasa from the road into the field and covers him with a garment. Once he is removed from the road, everyone continues to follow Joab in pursuit of Sheba son of Bichri.

❧ 2 SAMUEL 20:1-13

13

King David was now old, advanced in years, and though they covered him with bedclothes, he could never feel warm.

"A young virgin must be found for my lord the king," his courtiers said to him, "to care for Your Majesty, as his attendant. And let her lie in your bosom—then my lord the king will be warm."

So they looked for a beauty through the whole territory of Israel. They found Abishag the Shunammite and brought her to the king.

The girl was extraordinarily beautiful. She became the king's attendant and cared for him, but the king did not enter her.

1 KINGS 1:1–5

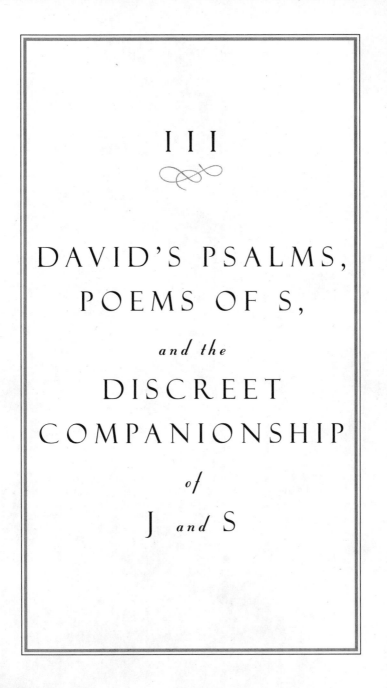

III

DAVID'S PSALMS, POEMS OF S,

and the

DISCREET COMPANIONSHIP

of

J and S

In addition to the psalm that illustrates this chapter, I have translated and will present ten additional psalms in the following chapter. All appear to have been edited or rewritten by S in the name of David—though it is possible David himself completed them in this form. They display the art of transforming a repressed history, in this case a lost history of indigenous roots. It takes a strong creative drive to keep such origins repressed, and the later Jewish traditions of creative transformation in Midrash, Talmud, and Kabbalah attest to it. It wasn't until this century, in the renewal of the Hebrew tongue as a modern language, that I found a new enthusiasm about linking to the primitive taproot. Although there was a movement of peripheral poets known as the "New Canaanites," the indigenous impulse expressed itself among many of the modern Hebrew poets, who felt they were recovering a sense of being rooted in the land. Freed of the repressive side to religion, they were probing history as individuals, on their own terms—and for a renascent Hebrew culture.

Perhaps the greatest of them was Avot Yeshurun, who died in his eighties only recently. Before we absorb the Bible's psalms in the light of S's knowledge of indigenous poetry, I want to present a few lines of Yeshurun's poetry to consider as a contemporary mirror. Looking into it, you may see the sensibility of an immigrant very different from the one who arrives in America. Yeshurun identifies first with the Bedouins, an imagined remnant of aboriginal tribes, and describes his fellow returnees so. "Yesterday" for Yeshurun was an aboriginal village.

> *The Bedouins who came from Poland not*
> *as planned spread out over Balfour*
> *Street opposite Ohel Shem now and on*
> *the slope opposite the sycamores now Nordia,*
>
> *And they were in tents and they were in huts and they were in*
>   *shacks.*
> *And a door handle about the width of a door and roofs.*
> *And roofs glided like children and changed.*
> *And summer and winter on Dizengoff Street.*
>
> *And all about rose up baronic houses.*
> *And domestic cedar spread out over the shacks.*
> *Tel Aviv holy city, you have no*
> *lullaby. Yesterday that was.*
>
> *I walked in you everything by foot,*
> *like the horse eats straight from the earth . . .*

> ❧ (from "Lullaby for Nordia Quarter," translated by
> Harold Schimmel, in *The Syrian-African Rift and Other Poems*,
> 1980)

Consider also the distinguished poet Leah Goldberg, who died in 1973, and worked—as S did three thousand years before—as a translator of world literature into the reflowering Hebrew language. Though she translated Shakespeare and Tolstoy, Goldberg wrote as an Indian princess restored to her ancestral land:

How shall we bring our dying heart up
To a new day as the light grows?
As when the wine bubbles in the cup,

As when the sky girds on his bow,
As when morning dances in the pit
And sunset bends to the river's cheek below,

And only we, by the terror bit,
Dream-robbed, witnesses from the fire saved,
Our blossoming land we will lift
Like a wreath of mourning unto the grave.

(from "On Blossoming," translated by Ruth Finer Mintz, in *Modern Hebrew Poetry*, 1966)

The Book of Psalms

If we project back three millennia we can imagine the Jerusalem streets paved by David and Solomon and walked by S one dawn, absorbing the sunrise as an aboriginal poet might have done many thousands of years earlier. The difference for S now is his self-consciousness, bounded by an awareness of a mirroring creator—with whom his psalm is in dialogue. Right away the indigenous oral poem is transformed by the poet's consciousness of his own hand writing, yet the memory of a boundless nature remains—"night listens" and the sun's rays are like words. Later in the poem, as the sun awakens in his tent like an aboriginal warrior, it melts into the presence of Yahweh, a consciousness of a boundless time and space.

Yet the whole psalm celebrates the transformation of an oral aboriginal poem into a consciousness of a written culture with libraries full of history scrolls. The "sweet flowing honey/ the right words/ in my mouth" recalls the primitive original, while the highly educated S sings of a cultural self-knowledge that is mirrored in writing: "we see the clear possibility/ of life growing/ to witness itself."

In this psalm, as others, we do not hear the voice of a newcomer to the land, but rather the restoration of a complete at-homeness, identifying the land with the entire universe.

Psalm 19

The universe unfolds
the vision within:
creation

stars and galaxies
the words and lines
inspired with a hand

day comes to us
with color and shape
and night listens

and what is heard
breaks through deep silence
of boundless space

the rays comes to us
like words
come to everyone

human on earth
we are the subjects
of light

a community
as it hears
the right words

creating time
the space of the sky
the face of the nearest star

that beats like a heart
in the tent where it sleeps
near the earth every night

then rises above the horizon
growing in our awareness
of the embrace

of inspiration
we feel as we turn
toward the warmth

starting at the edge of the sky
to come over us
like a secret love we wait for

love we can't hide
our deepest self-image
from

nobody holds back that fire
or closes the door
of time

words my Yahweh writes shine
opening me
to witness myself

sleeping and waking
complex mind
warmed in an inner lightness

that moves me
to the simple beat
of time

testimony
of one author
speaking through history's scrolls

commanding my attention
bathed in light
around me

clean perfect notes
hearts play
make us conscious

we become the audience
amazed we can feel
justice come over us

our minds become real
unfold
the boundless world within

silence becomes real
we hear
clear words

become the phrasing of senses
lines of thought
stanzas of feeling

more lovely than gold
all the gold in the world
melting to nothing in light

sweet flowing honey
the right words
in my mouth

warming your subject
as he listens
breaking through his reflection

his image in the mirror
what mind can understand the failure
waiting in itself

silent self-image
created in the dark alone
to hold

power over others!
but justice comes over us
like a feeling for words that are right

absolutely
a mirror is pushed away
like a necessary door

we're free to look at everything
every shape and color
light as words

opening the mind
from nightmares of social failure
desperate routines

we're inspired above
the surface parade
of men dressed up in power

we see the clear possibility
of life growing
to witness itself

let these words
of my mouth
be sound

the creations
of my heart
be light

so I can see myself
free of desperate symbols
mind-woven coverings

speechless fears
images hidden within
we are the subjects of light

opening to join you
vision itself
my constant creator.

❧   (from Psalms in *A Poet's Bible*)

The Book of Ecclesiastes

David no doubt wrote additional poems that were not included among the Bible's Book of Psalms, and we find traces of them in the Book of Proverbs and other biblical scrolls. In the Book of Ecclesiastes, which was composed in its final form many centuries later, we find quotations of earlier material, including a renowned poem whose celebration of the seasons suggests a deep, indigenous sensibility.

The questions the poetic text asks are of the kind associated with Solomon's quest for wisdom, yet the self-consciousness is Davidic, similar to Psalm 19. The poet describes his "own little creations" and frames it with consciousness of nature's creator, "in the awe of our hearts moving/ closer to their creator/ as we ourselves become stiller/ the grace to be still/ in the flow of all creation/ for a moment." It should be natural to consider the poem as aboriginal, tied to the seasons and to awe of nature's rhythms of life and death. Certainly it reflects a past rooted in the land.

If you suppress the irony and the poet's framing structure, one might think the following is simply a stoical proverb (though it is just as likely to be indigenous): "just to eat and drink/ the fruits of your work/ is a gift from your creator." But in fact the poet has played this off the image of himself as a creator, a creator of thought and poetry: It is his own poems that are the "fruits" he may "eat and drink." His creative profession may, in fact, provide real work. This is a level of self-consciousness I find typical of S, in the way this poem transforms an aboriginal wisdom into a Hebraic one.

There is time for everything to happen
under the sun   to lift anchor
in the flow of seasons

everything has its moment
under the uncounted stars
its season of desire

summer of being born
winter of dying
spring of seeding

fall of reaping
winter of killing
summer of healing

spring of uprooting
fall of rebuilding
fall of weeping

spring of laughing
winter of lamenting
summer of dancing

summer making love
winter of surviving
spring of embracing

fall of parting
spring of finding
fall of losing

winter keeping
summer discarding
summer of hot tears

winter of consoling
winter of silence
summer speaking out

spring in love
fall in anger
winter of war

and hating
summer of peace
and hugging

but what can a man add
to the interworking of things
of his own intrinsic value

is a man anything different
whether or not the sweat and thought
is wrung from his body like a rag

I have thought about the tatters
and felt the finest mindspun cloth
these are clothes created for us

all men and women wear them
the work of their creator
who has dressed everything in space

each event in time
tailored to its place
and he puts a maniken of desire

before the hearts and minds of men
so that we long to dress ourselves
create a vision of the future

in which our lives fit today
with a similar beauty of rightness
but the longing for a world of our own

defeats us   the world defeats us
like a mirror we may not look behind
though a taste of creation propels us forward

I have seen as with a long look
the best a man can make
is to create his own goodness

out of a clear image of himself
the satisfaction in simply being alive
the pleasure of his own eyes

seeing
as long as he can
as long as he lives

just to eat and drink
the fruits of your work
is a gift from your creator

the world is a gift that lasts
he gave
and nothing more can be added

no matter can be erased
the world behind us
came before us

and the wonder of our presence
is that we feel it all
in the awe before our own little creations

in the awe of our hearts moving
closer to their creator
as we ourselves become stiller

the grace to be still
in the flow of all creation
for a moment

and through the window of a moment
the opening of eyes within eyes
to see the ancient perspective of time

painted in a landscape with light
the future the eyelids opening
as of a prehistoric creature

under the ungraspable sky
that was
is

and will be: the airless height
of understanding   pure space we pursue
like fish the worms of conscience

and are drawn to
like a seed to air
in a new baby's wail

like a man to a woman
like a creature
to his maker.

(from Part V in *A Poet's Bible,* beginning at
Ecclesiastes 3:1)

The Book of Ruth

Finally, we consider the Book of Ruth. Some recent scholarship claims it was written after the fifth century B.C., reducing it to a social agenda of satire on Ezra's decree against mixed marriage. However, if it was written by J—as I suspect, along with many scholars who have judged it of Solomonic vintage—then the play between J and S is poignantly revealed here in all its profound tenderness. Naomi is transparently J, and the redeemer she is blessed with is her young protégé, S: "she became like a nurse to him." His name? Oved, meaning "assistant," or "worker." And, "he was the father of Jesse/ who was the father/ of David." The father of Jesse, for all intents and purposes, was an invention of S's—since it was he who gave him a lineage in writing. It is unlikely that much was known of David's real grandfather, any more than of his real mother—unless both their memories were suppressed. "Oved" is named by Naomi—or J—in S's multiple pun on the name, which also evokes humble origins.

Understood in this way, consider the irony of J/Naomi receiving a redeemer from her creator—in the form of her protégé and companion, S. Yahweh's "kindness" here resembles his lovingkindness in S's narrative. Here is S's mothering Yahweh reflected in J, providing her with a companion so that her work, her name, "will live on." We can also detect the sexual overtones of a relationship in the playful acknowledgment: "He will renew your spirit/ and nourish your old age." At the same time, we are not to miss the mirroring stories of Tamar in both J and S. Tamar's act of lovingkindness with Judah, in J's Genesis, is remembered here as a necessary boldness, a manifestation of Yahweh. Perhaps J wished to console S for the pain his own Tamar bore—and for her own jealous dotage upon him.

May your character reflect on Ephraim
your name live on in Bethlehem
your house grow as that of Peretz:
as he was born to Tamar and Judah
may Yahweh give to you
and this young woman
a seed that flourishes

So Boaz was pledged to Ruth
she became his wife
and he came into her

She conceived
and gave birth to a son
as Yahweh gave to them
a love that was fruitful

Then the women of the city
were saying to Naomi
Yahweh be blessed
whose kindness has not ceased
to this day, never leaving you
bereft of a redeemer

May his name live on
in Israel

He will renew your spirit
and nourish your old age
because he is born to the loving
daughter-in-law
who came beside you
and who has borne you more kindness
than seven sons

Then Naomi took the boy
held it to her breast
and she became
like a nurse to him—
the women of the neighborhood
gave it a name, exclaiming
a son is born to Naomi

The name they gave him was Oved
he was the father of Jesse
who was the father
of David

Now these are the generation
descending from Peretz:
Peretz and his wife gave birth to Hetzron
he to Ram, he to Amminidab
he to Nahson, he to Salmah
he to Boaz, he to Oved
Oved and his wife gave birth to Jesse
and he to David.

❧ (from the Book of Ruth in *A Poet's Bible*)

The sexual exuberance here, and underlying the entire text of Ruth—which pivots on the scene of Ruth giving herself at Boaz's feet on the threshing floor—has echoes of aboriginal fervor, transformed into a narrative of sublime restraint. And unmistakably, Ruth is a "Moabite" (which may have been a euphemism for an aboriginal, just as "Indian" is, mistaking one place for another) who transforms herself into a Jew in a shockingly simple manner. Could it really have been that simple and natural, especially when the religious sources are so agitated about mixed marriages? I believe that what makes it natural is that just as

Naomi is returning to her home, Ruth is also a symbolic exile, an aboriginal "Moabite" restored to overwhelming power. For it is Ruth's acceptance that makes it possible for a David to be conceived. And, we might add, for a David to be written into the Bible by J's companion, S.

There is also the image of Yahweh here as a mothering creator, secured in the background. This may represent the ultimate approval on J's part for her companion's biography of monotheism in the life of David.

IV

DAVID'S PSALMS

Transformations

I have continued to translate the psalms of David in the same manner as S himself might have done. They are transformations that mirror the imagination with which David founded his Hebraic culture.

The very first poem in the Book of Psalms is a love poem that transforms an indigenous song of isolation—and a sense of the outcast's outrage—into a conversation with a loving creator. Too many translations misrepresent the psalm by casting it in the light of righteous indignation. No, it is a love poem to the natural world, of being able to breathe freely in it. The sense of time here is the natural one between the planting of a tree and its fruiting—as opposed to the inflated pride that comes with human institutions, represented by a cafe and a papyrus scroll.

$\mathcal{P}$*s a l m   1*

Happy the one
stepping lightly over
papyrus hearts of men

and out of the way
of mind-locked reality
the masks of sincerity

he steps from his place at the glib cafe
to find himself in the word
of the infinite

embracing it
in his mind
with his heart

parting his lips for it
lightly
day into night

transported like a tree
to a riverbank
sweet with fruit in time

his heart unselfish
whatever he does
ripens

while bitter men turn dry
blowing in the wind
like yesterday's blemished scroll

unable to stand
in the gathering
light

they fall
faded masks
in love's firelight

burning hearts of papyrus
unhappily
locked in their own glare

but My Lord opens
his loving one
to breathe embracing air.

Among the best known psalms, Psalm 23 gives crucial evidence of the indigenous power that can reimagine and transform a culture built upon a pastoral past. The Hebraic culture idealized the shepherd, but the poet here transforms this idealization into an identification with the animal itself, the sheep. We feel the natural setting—grass, water, riverbank—more indelibly than the cities, in which isolation from the natural world is felt as pain. The poet who speaks is more human than his enemies because he is conscious of the origin of earth, air, water—and the natural sources of his food, even before animals were domesticated.

Psalm 23

The Lord is my shepherd
and keeps me from wanting
what I can't have

lush green grass is set
around me and crystal water
to graze by

there I revive with my soul
find the way that love makes
for his name   and though I pass

through cities of pain, through death's living shadow
I'm not afraid to touch
to know what I am

your shepherd's staff is always there
to keep me calm
in my body

you set a table before me
in the presence of my enemies
you give me grace to speak

to quiet them
to be full with humanness
to be warm in my soul's lightness

to feel contact every day
in my hand and in my belly
love coming down to me

in the air of your name, Lord
in your house
in my life.

Psalm 36 trusts love over the arrogance of the citified mind. This poem actually transforms mind into love—and lets the natural world stand for that love. By refreshing himself in indigenous roots, the poet is laying the basis for a new, highly developed culture of "gourmet fare" and of "eyes returning to mountains/ from the surface of the sea." He is "like any animal"—but in this case the poet has turned inside out the cliché in which animals are thought to be lower than humans. Human arrogance and male chauvinism are shown as mere strategems—"false faces"—beside the natural source of our origin: "the fountain of life." Just as the poet can speak to his creator, he can also become the creator in the poem of his interior consciousness, hearing it speak as well.

Psalm 36

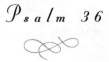

Inside my heart I hear
how arrogance talks
to himself without fear

hidden from eyes
he flatters himself
but we see him on the faces

of false faces and words
thinking—even asleep—
how to squeeze love out

from feelings from words
how to put wisdom on her back
and hold his miniature knowledge back

your love fills a man, Lord
with a kind of air
making him lighter

he rises in measure of your judgment
above the mountains of thought
above the clouds of feeling

the strength of his measure stays
in the eyes returning to mountains
from the surface of the sea

he falls like any animal
standing up only by your mercy
his children grow in the shadow of your wings

feast on gourmet fare in your house
with water that sparkles from wells
beyond the reach of a mind

the fountain of life
is lit
by your light

you extend your embrace
to those who feel you are there
keep holding the loving

keep us from being crushed
by arrogant feet
by the hand of pride

the powerful are falling over themselves
their minds have pulled them down
there they will lie, flung down.

An old, indigenous saying in Psalm 49—"prosperous men lose their intelligence"—is now turned into a great poem as it opposes a common Canaanite proverb about the fruits of prosperity—"So men may praise you in your prosperity." The seemingly advanced culture is shown to be hollow as the poet composes his transforming poem to the strains of his lyre. For all their means, the wealthy men of civilizations cut off from the natural world become merely meat, "stripped in death's store." Prosperity is transformed into imagination and withering irony by David's native intelligence.

All the civilized languages of Canaan are thrown into relief by the power of indigenous word-music, which is David's. Money becomes a symbol of "breeding"—but in this case the poet transforms the animal-breeding practices of Canaanite civilization into images of a narrow-minded piety. Once again David returns Hebraic culture to its roots in the natural earth.

Psalm 49

Now hear this, world
all who live in air
important, ordinary, poor

my lips are moved by a saying
my heart whispers
in sound sense

I measure with my ear
this dark message and it opens
around my lyre

why should I make fear
dog my steps
growl in my thoughts

when the masters of vanity
breed in public for attention
rolling in scraps of money

no man can build a way
to God outside his body
to buy his continual release

to pay a ransom in every moment
for the gift of living
the price higher than his power to think

so that he could live forever
blind to his own falling
into the pit of death

but we all can see
the wisest man dies
along with the cunningly petty

their fortunes pass like mumbled words
among others
above their graves

it is there in hardened silence
the inheritors will join them
their bodily measure of earth

and though they put their names
on spaces of land,
their inward thoughts like words,

the mouths wither around them—
prosperous men
lose their intelligence

remember that in its saying
like animals who leave nothing to quote
those men pass on totally self-centered

like sheep gathered into the earth
their followers headlong after them
death's herd

their flesh stripped in death's store
and the big show made standing upright
erased in the sunrise

but My Lord holds the ransom
for death's vain embrace
as this music holds me—inside

don't be afraid of the big man
who builds a house that seems to grow
to the pride of his family

nothing will lie between
his body with its pride
and the ground he falls to

the life he made happy for himself
"so men may praise you
in your prosperity"

will find the company
of his fathers
around him as total darkness

his inward thoughts like words
the mouth withers around—
prosperous men lose their intelligence.

In the following confessional poem, David transforms the temptations of civilization—"flattery" and "fame"—into the rewards of intimacy. In place of a world of immediate influence he finds the realm of other worlds outside himself. The shaman's world has been enlarged beyond cognition.

"My mind was useless" leaps beyond the shaman's song as David discovers the power to hear himself, a new level of self-consciousness. The poet has discovered that his own voice—its breath, music, and words—mirrors the cosmos. He learns that his creative powers are self-critical, and in trusting them they expand to parallel another creator—with whom his song allows him to intimately converse.

Here is another transformation of the signs of material prosperity into a wealth of imaginative intelligence—the burden of failure lightened, until the sky is revealed in its diverse blues.

Psalm 73

My Lord is open
to Israel, to all hearts
within hearing

but I turned and
almost fell   moved
by flattery spoken

through transparent shrouds
impressing me
with the power of imagery

and fame of the mind
loving to strut
in its mirror

with its unfelt body
smooth as a wheel
without a care in the world

prosperous mouthpieces
in their material chariots
of pride

and cloaks of status
covering up
crookedness

their eyes
are walls
for wish-images

their mouths big
cynical
trumpets

self-made gods
whose words envelop the heads of men
hiding their fears

they go through the world
in self-encasing roles
in which they will die

lowered in heavy caskets
they made themselves
out of words

but meanwhile they suck in
most people
draining their innocence

until everyone believes
God isn't there
no wonder these men prosper

they push through the world
their violence
makes them secure

it seemed I opened my heart
and hand
stupidly

every day had its torture
every morning
my nerves were exposed

I was tempted to hide
to kill the moment
with pride

instead I tried to know you
and keep your song alive
but my mind was useless

until my heart opened
the cosmic door
to a continual presence

that is you
lighting the future
above the highway

down which self-flattering men
travel in style
to prisons of mind-locked time

they have their pleasures
cruelly pursued
and you urge them

to their final reward
you let them rise on dead bodies
so they have to fall

like a bad dream
the moment you awake
they are gone forever

my mind was dry thought
my feelings drained
through dusty clay

I was blindly
eating through life
like a moth in wool

I was crude
too proud
to know you

yet continually with you
take my hand
in love

it sings with you
inspired advice
leading to your presence

what will I want
but continual inspiration
in the present with you

what else will I find
in the blues of the sky
but you

and me in you
where am I in what universe
without you

my body dies of exhaustion
but you are the mountain
lifting my open heart

higher than a mind can go
into the forever
into the future

men who hide in their hearts
have bitter minds
they will lose

those people become no one
leaving you for an ideology
for a material chariot

but I waited for you
I was open, My Lord
to find my song

I found you here
in music I continue
to hear

with each new breath
expanding
to give me space.

⌘

    David now imagines a conversation with his Lord in his own words. Reflecting on them, he thinks as the king he is, realizing that "all nations are men." The idea of the divine right of kings is stood on its head here, transformed into the power of an individual's words to create intimacy. The "lips/ smoothed by success" are transformed into the "silent critic"— in oneself and in others. The poet hears the call to speak in the name of all whose voices are suppressed by people "whose things enclose them." Again, the openness of a natural world supports an openness to self-criticism. But only a poet transforming the shaman's natural powers can help us see nations and "heads" of nations in ruins.

Psalm 82

⌘

My Lord is the judge
at the heart
in the infinite

speaking through time and space
to all gods
he let be

"instead of lips
smoothed by success
and appearances

defend your silent critic
locked in barred categories
his conscience

painfully opened
by vicious systems
release him

let him speak
break the grip
of the prosperous

whose things enclose them
from the lightness of knowledge
the openness of understanding

they build in darkness
burying justice
digging at the foundation

of earth and men
the orbit
of trust"

I was thinking
you too are gods
heads of nations

thoughts of my Lord
but you will disappear
like the spirit you silence

your heads fall
like great nations
in ruins

My Lord, open
their consciousness
to share your judgment

all nations are men
you hear
beyond categories.

In perhaps the strongest poem ever written, the poet's imagination itself becomes praise: He has transformed the shaman's imagination into a song of universal praise for life. Life is represented in its most natural form, the reproductive powers that bear us children. These are bound in the larger natural powers that create galaxies and universes, and within them "our minds are little stars/ brief flares." It is time, then, that the natural world reveals to the shaman, and to the transforming psalmist the timing of each written word and each breath have become the revelation of his own intimacy with life.

Foremost, there is the interior life, which is represented by a sense of the unconscious. Whether we are "eaten away/ with anxiety" or "worn-out swimmers," the imagery of natural processes is carried into our "little disasters" and our secrets from ourselves. All might end in "a sigh/ at the end/ of a story"—except that the natural universe is seen as a song or lyric that is always expanding. We forget this song of life is there and fall into "years lost in thought." Yet the intimacy with time is "your flowing"—to be enfolded in a process that includes both the moment and the act of "the work of this hand/ flowing open." The clichéd image of God's hand is here transformed into the poet's work, and the shaman's intimacy with the natural world becomes the poet's self-consciousness—and our own as well, as we mouth a creator's words.

Psalm 90

Lord, you are our home
in all time
from before the mountains rose

or even the sun
from before the universe
to after the universe

you are Lord forever
and we are home
in your flowing

you turn men into dust
and you ask them to return
children of men

for a thousand years
in your eyes
are a single day

yesterday
already passed
into today

a ship in the night
while we were present
in a human dream

submerged
in the flood of sleep
appearing in the morning

like new grass
growing into afternoon
cut down by evening

we are swept off our feet
in an unconscious wind
of war or nature

or eaten away
with anxiety
worried to death

worn-out swimmers
all dressed up
in the social whirl

you see our little disasters
secret lusts
broken open in the light

of your eyes
in the openness
penetrating our lives

every day melts away
before you
our years run away

into a sigh
at the end
of a story

over in another breath
seventy years
eighty—gone in a flash

and what was it?
a tinderbox of vanity
a show of pride

and we fly apart
in the empty mirror
in the spaces between stars

in the total explosion of galaxies
how can we know ourselves
in this human universe

without expanding
to the wonder that you are
infinite lightness

piercing my body
this door of fear
to open my heart

our minds are little stars
brief flares
darkness strips naked

move us to see your present
as we're moved to name each star
lighten our hearts with wonder

return
and forgive us
locking our unconscious

behind the door
and as if it isn't there
as if we forget we're there

we walk into space unawed
unknown to ourselves
years lost in thought

a thousand blind moments
teach us when morning comes
to be moved

to see ourselves rise
returning witnesses
from the deep unconscious

and for every day lost
we find a new day
revealing where we are

in the future and in the past
together again
this moment with you

made human for us
to see your work
in the open-eyed grace of children

the whole vision unlocked
from darkness
to the thrill of light

where our hands reach for another's
opening to life
in our heart's flow

the work of this hand
flowing open
to you and from you.

David's city, Jerusalem, is transformed in this poem into a state of mind. It is the writer's mind, in which a conscious creation is at one with the poet's intense awareness of his hand moving on the papyrus and his breathing. David also transforms the convention of invoking muses and gods; he beckons his inspiration while "no willful image/ blocks the door."

The writer goes further by mocking superficial attributes—"the theatrics of personality"—to reveal a deeper care for the personality, in the form of a new audience ("to share this space") open to self-knowledge. A self-critical love of character unveils clichés and "desperate images" as if they were part of a contrived dream—exposed by the inspiration of natural daylight.

This is probably David's strongest poem about a writer's need to transform his sources, an "imagination/ inspired/ by necessity." He opposes the conventional performance of "actors" to "love"—or an act of lovingkindness, which includes the writing of this psalm itself. But the ultimate contrast is to the openness of the natural world, here represented by light, wind, "real streets," and being at home in the cosmos: "won't you come to me?/ I sit here in my house." Home and the universe become one in Jerusalem, since David has unified them in a writer's self-consciousness.

Psalm 101

The city of your love
sings through me
before you, my Lord

you hold my writing hand
that makes my living
creative act

won't you come to me?
I sit here in my house
with an open heart

no willful image
blocks the door,
I just won't see

the theatrics of personality
crowding
the openness you allow

this art that hurts
those with ears for only jewelry
they go far away

locked within themselves
their self-flattery
I've reduced to silence

their narrow eyes
inflated pride
blown away

I'm always looking
for your people
to share this space

the contact of imagination
inspired
by necessity

beyond the stage doors
of weak characters
cut off from real streets

no more precious actors
costumed in sound
to litter this town with clichés

every morning
I silence with your light
desperate images

they run away
from the city of your name
that call an open heart.

The following great work of self-consciousness allows a deep intimacy with the *other*: David's God, woven into the texture of life even as he remains in the background. As the poet's creator, Yahweh provides the dimension in which self-creation can take place. But the author plays with and transforms the cliché in "such knowledge so high/ I can never reach with a mind" by the next line: "or hold any longer than a breath." He has identified the breath of life as the ultimate knowledge we need, and it is a mirror of creation.

Like a shaman, David goes on to identify his imagination with the sky, the sun, and other natural phenomena. His creator is vividly imagined at work—and he himself, the poet, is the work of art. And it is in this guise—as a created vessel—that the author can speak most intimately, venting his wounds: "stop the breath/ of men who live by blood." Yet the emotional knowledge he is after is self-critical and beyond anything shamanistic: "if any bitterness lives here/ lead me out/ into the self-less open"—even as that "open" has become one with the natural world. Life beyond time and beyond death is still imagined as bound within a natural creation.

Nature achieves its strongest unity with David and the Hebraic imagination in this great work, for nature itself is identified as a poet. It is easy to hear the shaman speaking through David now, and to hear how the poet transforms the imagery of nature—birds, sea, beach, stars—into "the great scroll of its life."

Psalm 139

∞

There's nothing in me, my Lord
that doesn't open to your eyes
you know me when I sit

you note when I arise
in the darkness closet of my thought
there is an open window of sunshine for you

you walk with me
lie down with me
at every move await me

at every pause
you know the words
my tongue will inscribe in air

if I say yes
you have already nodded
no—and you have shaken your head

in any doubts I lose my way
I find your hand
on me

such knowledge so high
I can never reach with a mind
or hold any longer than a breath

to get away from you
I could let my imagination fly
but you would hold it in your sky

or I could sleep with the dead in the ground
but your fire from the depths
would awaken me

I could fly on gold ray of sun
from dawn in east
west to stars of night

and your hand
would point the way
and your right hand hold me steady

however close I pull the night around me
even at midnight
day strips me naked

in your tender sight
black and white
are one—all light

you who put me together
piece by piece in the womb
from light

that work shines
through the form of my skeleton
on my song of words

you watched as my back steadied
the still-soft hull of ribs
in primitive workshop deep within

you saw me as clay
a life unfashioned
a craft at the bottom of the sea

and the great scroll of its life
this embryo will write
in a body you have sculpted

my Lord—your thoughts
high and precious
beyond logic like the stars

or like grains of sand I try to count
I fall asleep and awake
on the beach of your making

my Lord—stop the breath
of men who live by blood
alone and lie to your face

who think they can hide
behind the same petty smile
they use to smear your name

my Lord—you hear me hate
back your haters
with total energy

concentrated
in one body
that is yours and mine

my Lord—look at me
to see my heart
test me—to find my mind

if any bitterness lives there
lead me out
into the selfless open.

V

THE FIGURE

of

DAVID

*The Art of Leadership
in War and Writing*

The Art of Transformation

With his God moving to the background, David was free to embody human aspiration like a renaissance man. In fact, he was an inspiration to the artists of a later renaissance, such as Donatello and Michelangelo, who portrayed him as an inspiration as well. David's life was too broad to remain a religious paradigm; it was as complicated and ambivalent as a modern life. In the realm of power, or war, David projected leadership as an art that was balanced by the cultural art of writing. In the world of the mind, David's psalms remain the heights of poetry, while his life in maturity became transformed into art by the writer he directly inspired, the Court Historian of 2 Samuel, designated S.

With David as model, the art of leadership requires first and foremost a talent for transformation. Emotion and intellect—as war and writing, or culture—demand integration. David transformed the meaning of war and the meaning of culture by stressing their interdependence. Just as no Hebraic culture could have taken form without his war of independence, no biblical commentary and religion would have arisen without David's founding of a Hebraic renaissance and its writers of the Bible. To understand David's talent for transformation, it helps to first realize how his was not a birth of knowledge in the world, but a rebirth. Something profound needed to have preceded him.

We are approaching a time when we will begin to transform our vision of the future, but until now there has not been a daring view of the past in which to set the foundation. Archaeologists have taken the place of poets, yet without means to transform their insights into a creative vision. What is transformation? It is to take something lost or misunderstood, even outcast, and rediscover it as central to a new vision. As S recast the life of David in his writing, David himself transformed his memory of indigenous song into the first psalms written by himself or by S. In the same way, great works of art transform habits of thinking and feeling into a sense that more is possible, more life can thrive within us. But the loss that is transformed is deeply held.

At the bookends of our own century, the novelists Marcel Proust and Henry Roth transform the uses of memory. In his posthumous masterpiece *Mercy of a Rude Stream*, Henry Roth envisions contemporary Israel as a diverse culture parallel to David's original one. When his narrator delineates two reasons for living—love and a sense of creating something worthwhile—love's subtext is loss and the work that is created is a rediscovery of that loss in writing. Just as David's psalms were often written in a coming to terms with loss, Roth portrays his entire life as a war for the peace of mind that writing transforms. Neither writer allows hate to justify any action; their wars are a defense of love—which writing makes worthwhile, allowing a creative culture to blossom.

In ancient times, a defensive war was often fought to preserve an entire culture. If a city fell, its history and language might go with it. The wars of Saul and David, however, appear as those of a people who had been dispossessed of their land and who were fighting to restore it. The memory of the original loss was probably repressed, and in the place of a history of being outcasts arose a myth about a people of shepherds who went into slavery in Egypt. This myth culminated in a return to the Promised Land, a land newly consecrated to seem as if they had never been there before. The wars of Saul and David made this myth potent by creating the Hebraic culture for it to be written. Yet Saul still fought his wars on the old model of defending his tribal past, while

David fought to create a new culture that would assimilate the neighboring ones and revive a lost intimacy with the land.

This new way of waging war—not in defense of a culture but rather in defense of a new diversity that would change it—required a new art of leadership. David, poet and warrior, provided that authority for Israel and for the great biblical authors, J and S, who would come after him. The creative transformation of old realities into new forms of growth was David's genius. Not new forms—but forms of growth: David was the first forward-looking leader. The further into the future one looks, the deeper the past remains to be uncovered. David opened the way back to origins in the land—a way that was later covered over again when the stories of Abraham and Moses became fixed by a religious tradition that preferred commentary to a creative culture of writers.

Searching for the Original

Risk is not a quality approved of by traditionalists, which is why David and his biographer, S, are no longer figures of flesh and blood—as they were in the Renaissance for Michelangelo—but once again sublimated into a concept: messiahship. King David as an archetype of the messiah has become a safer topic among religion scholars than the man himself.

Unconventional ways of thinking can leave you wanting a protector. My search for a father figure led directly into the past and *The Book of J,* which ultimately taught me that I would have to recreate my own father figure. In the process—in my first explorations of the author S, J's companion—I began to realize that the life of King David, unlike other biblical characters, showed us the first model of a post-heroic figure in

Western culture. For David was reinvented by his author, S, to be a man who was not so much an original himself, but one who transformed himself. The original hero was a prehistoric shaman, but by David's time it was already too late for shamans.

How do we reimagine the original David? Not as a hero, but as a life reinvented by the Hebraic culture that David himself founded—only a post-heroic author could have written it. In David, S reinvented the shaman as a renaissance man. He was a holistic individual, we might say today, a man whose feminine side was not feared. He is neither half a man nor a holy man, but embodies the surprise of an individual who can think for himself. How do we trade the shaman's mask, which gives us the assurance of an accepted role—officer or professor, editor or celebrity, in today's terms—for a shield that shows our vulnerable face? Only with an open face can one be a discoverer, in the knowledge that the apparent weakness will also expose one's enemies.

When I read S's life of David, I could ask further: Why do the war scenes show a transformation into personal terms? The story is rarely about what you'd expect from a war history but always about the people, about personality. Whether it is a leader or a group, personality and culture are fused. It became apparent to me that David's shield would also tell a story of personality, and this became clear as I exchanged mask for shield in order to see my own life. Seeing oneself, one's enemies also are revealed. Saul, David's father figure and protector, became his worst enemy.

What David had to see was that Saul was the conventional authority, the heroic father. How can one be prepared for such a hero to become a danger? David had to learn his independent identity—fashioning a shield out of all he could learn from the Philistines and the outcasts while Saul, his former mentor, pursued him. We all have mentors who are masters of the past but are unprepared for the future. What our future says is: No single role, no one field of knowledge, is safe anymore. It's not enough to be a writer or a scholar, a president or a teacher, a scientist or a rabbi. Turn to the borders, the frontiers, as David did; turn to the outcasts, from whom you can learn your own losses. Leave the Sauls to pursue a heroic canon of the past. The time of cultural heroes is over; it is now the time to take up David's shield—not to take his place but to continue his war for learning from our enemies, and for independence of mind.

With a shield of my own, I was free to encounter the boundaries of convention. In our pasts the Sauls may wish us harm—as they wish to hold on to the past—but the shield serves to transform a king like David into a discoverer. What the old heroes accomplished by force, rein-venting themselves with power, now must be overcome with post-heroic self-knowledge, a probing of the borders of personality. To probe and learn—that is the essence of David's art of leadership—even when one's life has been uprooted. When David was uprooted by Saul, on the run and in hiding, he grew in stature as he learned new cultures and old resources among Philistines (or "sea peoples," a diaspora of Mycenaean Greece) and indigenous outcasts.

David Approaching Maturity

The way back to the original David has been prepared for us for some time through the efforts of Sigmund Freud in his essay "The Moses of Michelangelo." A figure of art and of history comes alive for Freud because he recognizes Moses as an "authored" figure. He shows us that knowing more about the artist Michelangelo or the Bible's authors does not mean feeling less; that inquiring into the origins of art and texts does not kill the stuff of life, but enlarges it. Michelangelo's marble statues of Moses and David reveal their author, Michelangelo, just as the Bible's Moses and David reveal their separate Hebraic authors. It was only in the

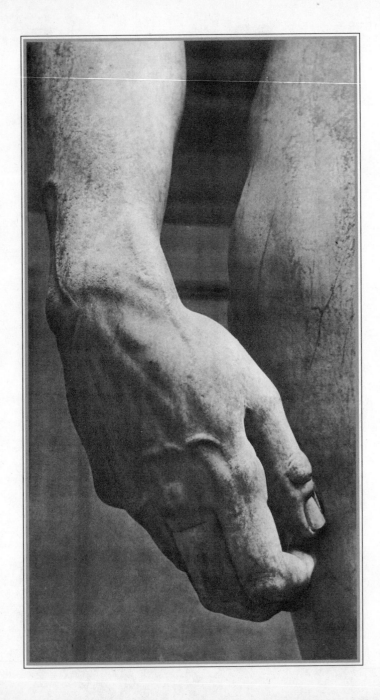

1930s in the book *Moses and Monotheism* that Freud would attempt with a figure of biblical text what he had done with a figure of art. However conjectural, Moses comes alive as a cultural figure with complicated origins and a complex sensibility.

When we look at the figure of David as written by the biblical author S, we see a similar transformation. David is a full-bodied, complex sensibility, one who can stand within himself and as part of something else—an army, a city, a culture, a story. And in another marble statue of Michelangelo's, one over sixteen feet tall, we have a literal figure of this David, not only full, but for extra measure large, pointing to a profound shift in Western consciousness. But in fact it was a rediscovery. In this David we get the sense that Michelangelo has rediscovered the figure of David, and that he has found his artistic counterparts, the biblical authors, in a much older renaissance. For many of us, when we think of David we first think of Michelangelo, perhaps even before the Bible, so that he becomes our stand-in for the repressed Hebraic renaissance of David's time.

On a sheet of some of his studies for the work of *David*, Michelangelo wrote a phrase from the opening of Petrarch's Sonnet 229: "Broken is the tall column and the green laurel." Michelangelo was envisioning a new definition of art and leadership. No longer would it be the idealism of unmarred, unbroken heroic columns and laurels upon the head—the beatific composure, the purity of origins and intentions. Now when we look at the face of his David, we see a cloudy brow of complex intensity, a face animated by ambiguities and conflicts. And we see an overwhelming power and readiness in the body of David, as our eye travels the route from legs to hands—one at his side in a repose of vulnerability, the other holding the sling in preparation for battle. Our gaze continues to the head and eyes directed at the site of battle.

At the center of all this is his sex, the matter-of-factness of David's genitalia. He is a new fruit that will bear even more new fruit, both as a man and as a leader, with one hand ready for war and the other one ready for intimate risk. The eye never ends its travel of the statue, propelled on by another hand, that of the artist, who held his tools as an extension of himself—just as the sling seems almost a part of David's hand. Written on the same sheet with the quote from Petrarch: "David with the sling and I with the Bow. Michelangelo." The bow is the instrument that was used with the sculptor's drill.

David's sling almost seems like an instrument for art as well as war in the statue, and in it two figures and their art are fused: the promise of David's art and that of Michelangelo's, for this statue was created by him at the beginning of his career and David is poised at the beginning of his own. This is the David before the "City of David," but the promise and the sorrow are already in the statue. The figure of David that would build that city and embody it will exchange the sling for the shield in the Western imagination.

Just as we can use the sling to imagine the young David of the legendary battle with Goliath, we can use the shield to reimagine the mature David, the David of S. While there is a long tradition of using the shield (or Star of David) to depict his religious or metaphysical attributes, David's original Hebraic culture has been repressed. No one has utilized David's shield to reveal the figure of David—his character and personality—as developed by his original author, S, in 2 Samuel. There, David is a singular figure created by a single author, and his shield comes to represent a uniting of dual realms: character and author; literature and history; culture and nation; writing and religion.

THE WHOLE MAN

David's Shield

David's life dramatizes how emotion and intellect can't be integrated until our wounds and failures have became part of our emotional knowledge. It was this knowledge that led me to translate S, or the Court Historian, as a discrete, ancient masterpiece for the first time. Although Harold Bloom agreed that S's writing produced our first great novel, he was not enamored of it. I understood that there was little new for him to say after he had described J as the strongest and uncanniest biblical writer. S was a writer who could portray weakness, loss, and intimacy, which were also the qualities of David's psalms. The best original psalms reveal an emotional strength more than an intellectual one. It is the kind of emotional intelligence that is humbling and cannot be found without the integration that David's shield represents.

The shield allows its holder to be vulnerable, post-heroic. Flaws that need to be hidden in the past—defects of will and intellectual strength—can be transformed into creative strengths by holding the shield. The poet in David becomes emblematic for our time as well, when the wish to be a poet is still alive. Yet many poets overlook David's psalms—and they still resist the natural and aboriginal sources of pre-historic cultures. Like the psalms, indigenous poetry prefers an older, natural history over the recorded history we cling to. The shaman's song submits to other species, to jaguar, to antelope, and to trees as power-fully imagined beings; it embraces far more of evolutionary history than Western culture does.

As in every human discipline, there are great shamans and ordinary ones. The great shamans of prehistory transformed their weaknesses into a form of imaginative submission to natural history. In David's psalms and in his mature life as written in the Bible by S, we find that same ability to submit to an imagined father figure, a singular God. And for the first time in Western history, God moves to the background: David is content to speak for himself, and to interpret his imagined father's desire for himself as well.

Embodying the Shield

David's character is almost as complex as evolutionary history, and as intricate as a modern sensibility. To interpret it, David's shield can become a figure of insight. The layered triangles diagram qualities we can better understand by laying them side by side and learning to embody them. S enfolds these aspects of character in David's life. Mystics have unfolded them in the past, but this only made David seem more removed from everyday life.

The lower triangle of the hexagram star contains the qualities of emotional knowledge, and the upper triangle the modes of activation or intellect. The entry point of intimacy, on the lower triangle, becomes active by its inverse and highest point on the upper triangle, leadership. All three points on the lower triangle of emotional knowledge need their corresponding points on the upper triangle of intellect to make them active.

UPPER TRIANGLE

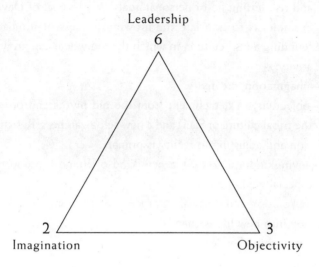

Leadership
6

2
Imagination

3
Objectivity

LOWER TRIANGLE

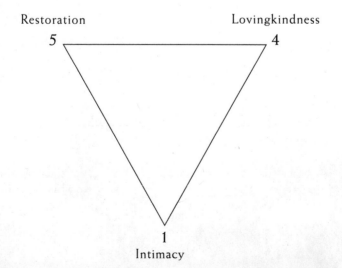

Restoration
5

Lovingkindness
4

1
Intimacy

1—intimacy. It is a model of being able to fall in love, as David does, and risk letting go of personal goals. A new goal of David's, for example, is to translate the growing process of intimacy into founding a new culture, in which the individual can grow in creativity.

2—imagination, creativity.

3—objectivity: a detachment from the old myths and order (e.g., the tribal culture of Saul) and a new self-awareness. Resisting illusion and adjusting to reality is primary.

4—lovingkindness (*chesed*), a new kind of friendship and respect, especially among nations.

5—restoration and renewal. A process of mourning and its translation into new life is enacted.

6—leadership. The leader creates a new audience.

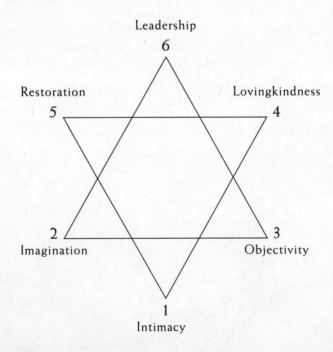

Each point applies to both war and writing. In war, each point embodies a sense of how to relate to others. In writing, each point embodies a sense of how to relate to oneself.

The fourth and fifth qualities, which complete the lower triangle of emotional knowledge, are lovingkindness and restoration. Lovingkindness is stimulated by the second point on the upper triangle of intellectual knowledge, imagination. In the same way, the fifth point on the lower triangle, restoration, becomes active by means of objectivity, which is the third point on the upper triangle.

Intimacy is the entry point, the first point on David's shield, at the bottom of the lower triangle. This quality of intimacy begins with harmony—a harmonious balance with nature that is derived from the aboriginal culture in David's ancestral background, a culture intimate with its environment. "Professors of the forest" is how I have described that original culture's shamans. It was a culture still alive in David's time, though they were called "outcasts." Yet these were the same people David trusted with his life before he became king. These outcasts, who helped save David from the murderous King Saul, still lived with their origins—their trees—rather than in cities, and they probably considered the city people to be the true misfits in the land.

David learned a personal intimacy from the indigenous people's environmental intimacy. This intimacy made crossing boundaries easier, just as living with a diversity of species was a natural condition. David crossed boundaries of love and affection as a leader, and the art of his leadership projects a strong personality in war that is at the same time sensitive to an enrichment of culture. Writing is symbolic of that culture, as it translates knowledge of the past and assimilates it among a new diversity of citizens. David's time stood at a great crossroads, where the old cuneiform writing was being translated and transformed into the early Hebraic alphabet.

Since the second and third points appear on the upper triangle, together with the sixth, we move directly from intimacy to the fourth and fifth points of emotional knowledge, which are on the lower triangle of the shield.

Lovingkindness, or *chesed*, is the fourth point on David's star. It remains the next point on the lower triangle because it's a quality of emotional knowledge that needs to be stimulated by an active agent of the upper triangle. Lovingkindness is what David shows to his neighbors right from the opening sentence of S's narrative: "Is there no one left from Saul's family—one to accept my lovingkindness?" After showing love to the lame son of Jonathan, David reaches out further, ready to show lovingkindness to the son of Nachash—Hanun—an Ammonite king. When David is rejected, it is the concept of lovingkindness itself that is rejected. For David's alliances go deeper than agreements of interest; they show deep interest and respect for the neighbor's culture. Enemies, too, are known and understood by their cultures and how those cultures have treated others. When the Aramaeans are defeated, they "turn away from the extended hand of the Ammonites"—Ammon extended its hand, but not true lovingkindness.

The leader in war embraces his army and nation with lovingkindness, as if they are his family. "Look upon your soldiers as beloved children," wrote Sun Tzu in *The Art of War*, the Taoist classic written six or seven centuries after David's death—and David had actually treated his army in that manner. His role as father of the nation or culture is paralleled by God's fathering toward him: a willingness to step back and let creativity assert itself. What kind of emotional vulnerability is this? It is a transformation of weakness—it is only because David knows his own flaws that he can embrace faults in others.

Similarly, if one feels lovingkindness toward one's sources in writing, they will prove to be the roots by which a work may last. Virtuosity, on the other hand, dies with its generation, because in it, emotional knowledge remains undeveloped—and intellectual insights are soon enough replaced with the new and latest fashion of thought. The biblical works associated with David bear this out: The original psalms in their loving transformations of their sources, and the court history of David by rooting itself in David's character. Yet lovingkindness, the fourth point on the lower triangle, requires the second point on the upper triangle, imagination, to become active.

This second point overall, imagination, is also the entry to the upper triangle. In S's great writing of the scene, David's loyalty is first to the intimacy he has created with Bathsheba; the loyalty of her husband, Uriah, on the other hand, remains toward his superiors. David and Bathsheba demonstrate an intimacy based on equality, where authority resides within the power of the intimacy itself. Lovingkindness is here, and in the imagination that rescues it. Imagination reveals the relationship with Bathsheba, which will yield the king's heir, Solomon, as a natural flaw, or vulnerability, that can be atoned for. Imagination allows the first step, to keep the truth alive.

Only the unimaginative commentators will miss the power of S's writing here; these conventional commentators go on to suppose that S intended to insult David, for political purposes or for religious reasons, such as his unpriestly behavior. But prosaic thinkers lack the emotional knowledge to embrace the whole man, good and bad. They fail to understand the writer's subtlety in revealing a sensitive David, both poet and warrior.

In *The Art of War*, Sun Tzu writes, "be extremely subtle," for the advantage of enigma is crucial to the leader in war. David's imagination is similar in spirit, defying ordinary expectations. The element of unconventionality is a characteristic of David's leadership, even in his mode of mourning—as in the loss of his son by Bathsheba, and, later, the loss of his son Absalom. These losses become imaginative transformations of emotional knowledge.

From his ancestral culture, represented by the outcasts who were his trusted cohorts, David derived objectivity—the third point on his shield—that allowed him to restore (fifth point) intimacy and establish a new culture. The psalms of David are further evidence, translating a natural intimacy into the most intimate relationship: that of a man and his God, to whom he speaks objectively, as an interpreting subject. The psalms turn a poetry of knowledge of the land into a poetry of "action": an imagined conversation with the nonhuman.

Suddenly, what used to be the elite world of the shamans is made personal and democratic for all in the poetry of the psalms. Here is the origin of personality in Western culture, a transformation of aboriginal space into personal interiority. We are made witnesses to it in David's actions, which stretch the borders of personal experience. Just as we become intimate with his creator—as readers of David's psalms—we also become intimate readers of David's interior life when he speaks to our experiences of love and attachment.

Objectivity, the third point overall, is on the upper triangle and requires the emotional knowledge of restoration on the lower triangle: Our losses have to be admitted so that intimacy can be restored. Objectivity also suggests the Taoist classic on war. Sun Tzu writes that the calm, detached warrior wins, and "those who celebrate victory are bloodthirsty, and the bloodthirsty cannot have their way with the world." David's greatest strength is his intelligence, founded upon his restoring the origins of his Hebraic culture in the land. His objectivity about himself and the past allowed him to be involved in relationships with all the neighboring cultures, and his life demonstrates intimate knowledge and alliances with even his worst enemies, from the Philistines to his own King Saul. A love for these cultures is evident in the way their works are assimilated into the Hebraic culture by writing— including the Mycenaean Greek forms of narrative underlying the Philistine culture, and the transformations leading to the Hebrew alphabet. The Hebraic culture that David nurtured was based upon a symbolism of "twelve tribes," which probably represents the diversity of cultures in Israel at that time, from the remnants of indigenous Hebrews, to the settled Canaanite colonists, to the migrating cultures from Egypt and Mesopotamia.

The fifth point overall, restoration, searches out forgotten bonds and renews them. Losses are mourned and transformed by renewal. David explains to his startled courtiers why he stopped mourning his son's illness when he died: "Now that he is dead, what is the use of fasting? Can I bring him back again? I may go to him, but he can never come to me." And then: "David consoles Bathsheba, his wife; he goes to her and lays with her; she bears a son whom she named Solomon." The transformation yields a healthy son: "and Yahweh loved him."

On the lower triangle of emotional knowledge, restoration requires an understanding of mistakes made. This knowledge comes in the process of mourning the losses that these mistakes make inevitable. Was it a mistake to pursue father figures who, like Saul, would reject their imagined heirs? David mourns it, and the mourning process leads to objectivity: the third point on the upper triangle, and the agent by which restoration can be enacted. When David acknowledges and mourns his mistakes, he is able to harbor ambivalence and sustain the complexity a great culture will need. S, the creator of David's character in the Bible, shows us the process of his own ambivalence toward his role as writer and historian of the Davidic court by stretching his role into one of a creator: His written life of David in fact objectifies—as it atones for—David's mistakes. David becomes the object of his own *chesed*, or lovingkindness. The writer, in his active agency as creator of Hebraic culture, is what has allowed God and religion to move to the background. From this point on, religion will become again a separate sphere of culture, just as it was in the indigenous religions upon which S draws—and as it resembles the Western history of secular cultures.

Restoration, and the accompanying objectivity, free the memory: David restores the land to its original state, a prehistory when the indigenous Hebrews saw themselves as tenants and tenders of the

ecosystem, like most indigenous tribes. Now, in his imaginative transformation, the Hebraic culture that David founds is not so much the
owner of the land, but the tenant of their Creator, the monotheistic
God. The land becomes a metaphorical Promised Land, and the old
hymns of praise become transformed into David's psalms of direct relationship to the creator.

Further, the aboriginal forest is recreated in cultural terms as a *library*
to draw upon and an *archive* with roots in the past. What had represented
the outcast before—living in direct relationship to nature—is transformed into a human nature, a new consciousness of being in relationship to the origins of nature.

Finally, the leader creates a new audience by means of integrating
all these points. Both an army and a culture are redefined by the force
of a leader's sensibility: his way of relating to himself. David related to
himself as a son—not so much to his natural father, of whom we hear
little, but by creating his own father figure: a model, a shining exemplar,
a figure of such dominance, it can step back and relinquish a need to
dominate, allowing a renaissance of culture to flower.

Restoration, the fifth point, has led directly to the the sixth and
crowning point, leadership. It was accomplished through writing, which
transforms daily life and its speech. The unmediated power of spoken
words, in life as in dreams, is what great writing recalls. Words spoken
directly to us. We know they were spoken because the power of memory and art can restore a world in which such speaking is possible. For
King David, the leader, a world of intimacy with the land is restored by
a culture that recreates it in writing. The Hebraic writers of the Bible will
elaborate the story of the "Promised Land" beginning with J's great narrative in Solomonic times. David's founding of that Hebraic culture was
a goal worth fighting for. Leadership in war and leadership in writing—
the foundation of Hebraic culture—are mirror images of each other.

2

BACKGROUND

History of the Shield of David

What repressed power does David's shield—or the six-pointed Star of David—hold in the twentieth century? It so enraged much of the gentile world that German-occupied Europe branded each individual Jew with it as a sign of the outcast. Yet the Star of David was not a sign of aggression for Jews. Instead, it signified the sublimation of aggression into cultural creativity, gracing Jewish artifacts that ranged from Hebrew schools to greeting cards, sometimes with the word *shalom* within it. *Shalom*, or peace, is a fundamental Jewish concept—probably deriving from the same source as the city of David, Jeru*salem*. As Christianity took hold in the West, Jewish concepts like *shalom* and the cultural meaning of Jerusalem as David's capital (apart from its religious meaning) seemed to be superseded. However, not only would the Jews not go away, but Jewish culture thrived in exile, and the Star of David has gone through creative transformations that range from the medieval Kabbalists to the flag of the state of Israel. Its power also precedes the Christian cross and such later signs as the Christmas star.

Our best authority for the origin of the Jewish star or shield of David (*Magen David* in Hebrew) is Erwin Goodenough, whose major study of Jewish symbols encompasses eight volumes written in the 1950s. Goodenough brings the culture of Hellenistic Jewry to life as never before, revealing its inherent genius for transformation. Gershom Scholem, the renowned scholar, also shaped his life's work around a project of uncovering the repressed power of Jewish culture—in his case, in the Kabbalah. Both Goodenough and Scholem discover a past that was nearly unrecoverable in the twentieth century; in the same spirit of revelation, historian Lucy Dawidowicz called the Second World War "The War Against the Jews," even as a regeneration of Jewish culture in Israel follows.

Three thousand years ago, David's kingdom was also founded in a time of war. Like modern Israel, its focus was on creating a new language and a new culture. As we become conscious of the value in cultural diversity, it is bracing to discover that the inhabitants of David's Israel prized diversity in several ways. A household, for instance, might consist of wives and their relatives from numerous cultures, and the traditions of each were honored. In the king's household and at his court, the education of thousands of the elite would require reading and writing in many languages—and, above all, the translation from cuneiform and other scripts into the newly adopted alphabet. Building a culture entailed an enriching of the language: The greater the diversity of sources, the more fertile it became.

David was the harbinger of a return to indigenous sources in the wealth of the land because he nurtured the resources of the new Hebraic culture. Essentially, David became emblematic of the richness in each individual—richness of tradition behind him and richness of potential before him. A boy of humble stock could rise not only to power but to the worldliness of great poetry and schooling. The embodiments of David's reign were not religious accomplishments but the cultural institutions he founded, the libraries, the love for scrolls and tablets. And in these David enshrined most deeply the love of nurture, of bringing out the full range of diverse origins in others. It is a nurturance of diversity and complexity, and it is reflected in the life of David as written by the author whom scholars have long called the Court Historian, although the court at which he wrote was more likely to have been Solomonic.

By Solomon's time, the seeds David planted had blossomed extravagantly. Solomon built dozens of shrines in the traditions of his diverse foreign wives, and these shrines were a lasting legacy to Israel, protected for many centuries.

Although the Shield of David is the most popular emblem of David today, its origin as a sign of salvation is not well known. Unlike the Christian cross, Jewish salvation was intimately bound up with the culture David founded. Scholem believed that the Star of David, as it is popularly known today, was a repressed aspect of Jewish history that was rediscovered by Jewish Kabbalists and alchemists who transformed Arabic magic in the Middle Ages. Yet its association with David was based on the sense of his protecting influence. More intimate than a star, it became again the shield protecting David: both as an aspect of his personality, something that he carried close to him, and the source of his own protection, the God behind him.

Goodenough determines the shield descends from an ancient six-petaled rosette known as the "banal" rosette, and that rosettes were typical signs of royalty in the ancient world long before the Hebraic culture in Canaan. Scholem is probably right that the shield's history as we know it today—the *Magen David*—began with the medieval Kabbalists, for whom it was a sign of protection, yet it was found in Jewish use a millennium earlier, in the Hellenistic era. As much as the Kabbalah contains repressed traditions of Judaism, I would venture that for David himself the shield represented a return to aboriginal origins, the naturalism of the petals transformed into the cultural dimension by the doubled triangles. For David was no typical royal conqueror; instead, his character was symbolic of a new Hebraic culture founded on the complexity of personality.

There is no court without a king, and the court history of David was written by an author trying to solve the problem of repressed origins and the loss of David's vitality. For S, the Court Historian, was writing at the court of Solomon's son, Rehoboam, and the creative culture of David and Solomon had already entered into eclipse. What sets the court history of S apart from the other stories about David in the books of Samuel is that S constructs the first novel in Western history to present David as our primary personality, who can himself—without God's intervention—transform a people's life and keep alive their origins. David is the second creative force in the Bible after God himself. Not only has David created himself, as S depicts him, but S himself becomes a creator in his own right: Both have found a way to transform loss into the founding or revival of a culture—born in war and writing.

War Process and Peace Process

Questions about the origin of war persist today, and they are answered in ways similar to the way they were in the time of S. Writing to Einstein in the years leading up to the Second World War, Freud answered Einstein's question about why we have war. He argued that we are capable of transforming our ways of organizing aggression into creative cultural pursuits, such as writing. Both pursuits—war and writing—are processes, according to Freud, and we may go further: War is also a process toward peace, and writing, a creative process. In war, David shows how aggression can be transformed into a process of forming friendships—a peace process—and how creating peace among men and nations allows God to move into the background. In the same way, the creator is transformed into the creative process itself when David revives Hebraic culture.

"Whatever fosters the growth of culture works at the same time against war," wrote Freud. To define culture, Freud described the transformation of aggressive impulses into the strengthening of the intellect and interior life.

Almost three millenniums earlier, this is exactly how S presented David in his written creation of the mature king's life: A distinctive personality is characterized by an interiority. From the beginning, David is shown on his palace rooftop to have an internal life, in the midst of thinking to himself, when he first sees Bathsheba. And in the very beginning of his work, S shows David embodying the process of *chesed*, or lovingkindness, as a *peace process:* taking care to attend to the repair of broken relations. Over and over again, in the midst of war, David returns to the dispensing of lovingkindness. War can also be waged with a desire to create a method for a productive peace. Reconciliation brings the means to foster the creative process—and writing stands as the central embodiment of that process in Hebraic culture, prefiguring the Jewish love of learning.

If Michelangelo had created David in his mature years, as S has done in his novel of David's life, it would begin in a similar place, showing David's act of lovingkindness in the midst of war. Michelangelo created a mature Moses, holding the tablets, and a mature David would hold the shield, showing the extension of his influence into the culture. What would the shield look like? Yet here we can stop speculating—for we already have the symbolic or abstract representation of it in the Shield of David. As an abstraction, it also represents a more complex transformation as it becomes symbolic of the creative process—a creativity that is the fruit of the peace David has been fighting for. Rather than a shield to use in battle in appearance, it is abstracted into a figure whose meaning is coterminus with David's personality.

When Scholem asked himself "What does the Shield of David mean?" he could answer only that there was none known outside of magic. Since there was no religious meaning, the cultural use in Zionism could be oriented to the future: The star was a creative surface. And at its most creative it echoes the ancient Hebraic culture in its first renaissance: that of the Bible's original writers. Now, by returning to the inspiration of that Hebraic culture and its writers—whose written art was as strong as Michelangelo's visual one—we can begin to discover the qualities of leadership in David that lie behind his shield.

David Writing

As great as was his 1920 philosophical masterpiece in German, *The Star of Redemption*, Franz Rosenzweig could not free himself of the fear of individuality. He took the emblem of David's shield and its separate triangles, giving each of the six points a path or element of a theology. David himself was unimportant to him except as a footnote to the messianic concept. But with a recent growth in knowledge, it is possible to uncover the repressed individual and return to the original authors. So I've given back to David his psalms and also his shield, as a symbol of his complex humanity and his founding of a Hebraic culture.

Like most biblical experts, Rosenzweig thinks in terms of politics and religion—as if the totality of culture did not exist beneath, above, and around them. Since David appeared not to be a theologian or philosopher, the interest in him has been largely confined to his political influence. The great author of his life in the Bible's 2 Samuel—the Court Historian, or S—is read merely as a political history. Perhaps because Rosenzweig came too early in the century to acquire an analytic psychology, he does not wish to see himself fully as an individual—except in contrast to a communal "we." In the same manner, David for him is reduced to an agent, deprived of being his own man. Yet it becomes evident in S's masterpiece that David had his own psychology, based in indigenous culture, and that he had a strong sense of himself as an individual.

I have come to see David's shield in a more personal way than previous writers did. Franz Rosenzweig, for example, does not even refer to S because he is so intent on grounding himself in communal concepts. He cannot admit a singular author, just like the critics still writing today, who will be examined in the appendix to this book.

According to Scholem, the shield is a perfect symbol for repressed material. And what was—and still is—the most repressed aspect of Judaism is its original Hebraic culture. Only in 1897 did the Shield of David acquire a new association as the symbol of the Zionist movement, which aimed to return the Jews to their home in Israel—but also to recreate Hebraic culture, beginning with a revival of the Hebrew language. The Shield of David thus became a return of the repressed.

Writing in 1949, a year after the rebirth of Israel, Scholem explains that David's shield, "the sign that in our days was sanctified by suffering and torture, has won its right to be the sign that will light up the road of life." As in several of David's psalms—"Where it was humbled, there will you find it exalted"—it is a sign of transformation. Now it is a symbol again of creating a culture. The bias against this Hebraic culture in the past is perhaps best summed up in Mircea Eliade's sixteen-volume *The Encyclopedia of Religion* (1987). This exhaustive resource refers to David's psalms as "originally anonymous," although nowhere in the Bible is there a hint about anonymous persons. Even the experts who examine the great cave art of prehistoric humans—as much as thirty millenniums older than the Hebraic culture of David—do not assume the original artists were unknown to their contemporary culture. Yet few scholars today are concerned about what happened at the origins of Hebraic culture. Like most standard sources, Eliade's encyclopedia can describe S's court history only as a political ploy—in this case, to make David look bad by humanizing him!

The memory of a unique writer such as S, who stretches the boundaries of his genre like all great artists, is worth rescuing. S's genre is history, and to say that he is no ordinary historian is beside the point. S was a transformer, a genre-bending artist of the word. Today we might call him a novelist. Yet our novelists today are so inseparable from their genres that none are likely to be looked back upon as our great historians.

David was a warrior and a writer. This crucial synthesis requires a talent for transforming the warrior's heightened awareness of being vulnerable into poetry and self-knowledge. In effect, David's psalms were confessions of the corrupting desire for power as well as songs of praise to the creative spirit. Both as confession and song, they heighten awareness of being in relationship to an unknown listener. They are, in essence, shamans' poems, the writer self-aware that he is in relationship with the unknown. Especially in the confessional psalms, relationships with others are examined for their dependency, as if the shaman-poet is in need of self-knowledge.

David has transformed the shaman's role: Now it is the individual who is in relationship with the source of his creative power. This allows David's psalms to become songs of love, of unburdening intimacy with a creator or Lord. And the life of the mature David—written by S, who perhaps rewrote some of the psalms as well—reveals a transformation into historical narrative of what had previously been confined to the realm of legend.

V I

IN SUMMATION

A Personal Note

In Summation: A Personal Note

This book, *The Book of David*, goes beyond the work that I published with Harold Bloom in 1990, which we called *The Book of J.* Instead of a companion work, it is about the work of companions who were also colleagues and great biblical authors in an ancient renaissance. These two authors and their beloved King David shaped more than the culture and consciousness of the Jewish people: They provided the bedrock for Western civilization as well. Behind the figure of David is the story of his biographer, S—known to us in the books of Samuel as the Bible's "Court Historian"—and his companionship with J, the author who is conjectured to have written the foundation of Genesis and Exodus.

Chapter V, entitled "The Figure of David: The Art of Leadership in War and Writing" is based upon the investigation that precedes it. The realization that David is the shared inspiration behind the writings of both J and S is here transformed. Without David, the Bible could not have been written. And without the unique relationship between David and his God, the drama of Jesus and his Father would have lost its biblical model. In the same way, the power we have to shape our individual lives today would seem less significant. Without David we would lose our strongest idea of an interior life.

Throughout this book I have based my speculations upon the facts that are deducible from the Bible and the latest scholarship about the history of its writing. I began with what is left to us of S's work and is considered to be contained in chapters nine to twenty of 2 Samuel of the Hebrew Bible. Like J, S wrote with a sensibility that has endured through all the traditions of redaction and commentary that came after the great secular culture founded by King David. And also like J, S expanded the boundaries of what could be written and imagined. He and J were intimate companions in the artistic and literary restorations characteristic of the court of David's son, King Solomon, and of the court of David's grandson as well, King Rehoboam.

Although David had just recently died, something more was already lost by the time of the authors J and S. That story of loss and its transformation by two of our Western culture's greatest but most forgotten writers is the one I have told. In alliance with J, his mentor and companion, and other lost writers, S made himself into a profound literary artist: He became the biographer of monotheism by authoring the life of David.

In my notes on the translation of J in 1990, I wrote, "More than translation, a reconstruction of the Book of J should risk sensitivity to the original narrative voice." It was during this process of translating J and realizing her unique voice that I became aware she was part of a culture and that she had peers and colleagues. At first I thought her peers might be writers whose work had been expunged like much of J's own. I had been aware for some time of the audacious art of the court history in 2 Samuel and the parallels with J that had been advanced by Bloom and an older generation of biblical scholars. But I didn't know how to imagine a culture in which writers as diverse as J and S could be intimate colleagues.

The groundwork began with *The Lost Book of Paradise*, the book I undertook after *The Book of J*. There, I focused exclusively on the origins of Hebraic culture, through the myth of the story of Adam and Eve in the Garden of Eden and its recovery as a lost scroll. My guide was an imagined translator in the court of King Solomon, and though I still did not have in hand another author as dynamic as J, I found a crucial hint during the writing of *The Lost Book*. I realized that S had to have been another writer in a renaissance culture of courtiers who were brought up in the study of many languages and cultures. That is, the culture of S had to be a renaissance culture—one that was reclaiming and restoring an extraordinary past.

But what could that past have been? That question and the more significant questions about how a forgotten and lost past could be transformed led me to understand that the Book of David was a work of creative transformation by a genre-bending genius, a writer such as had never before been recognized. In past scholarship, it was history, apology, and even "a great story" that have been acknowledged in the court history of S. Yet it has eluded recognition as an uncanny and great work, which, like all great works, expands the boundary of its form. Since I already had experienced such an author in J, I now had found the equivalent of her companion. And I had the beginning of the proof that I needed of a culture of biblical writers who provided the fertile soil in which the transformation of the gods of the land into monotheism would take root.

It was at this point that I felt I had to know more about the aboriginal cultures that were at the origin of the Hebrew tribes. I talked with scientists in the field. One ethnobotanist in particular, Professor Brad Bennett, helped me to understand how complex an aboriginal culture can be—even more than our own—and how misunderstood it has been until very recently. At the same time, my research in Jerusalem provided the archaeological and linguistic support I would need to imagine Solomonic Jerusalem.

During one of my research expeditions I took some time out with Philip Rieff, the world-renowned sociologist, to make a journey to a unique five-star hotel in a suburb of Jerusalem. We knew that it had been evacuated and newly set aside for several thousand immigrants arriving from Ethiopia, most of whom had never before seen a toilet, a lightbulb, or a piano. Professor Rieff, who tended to be skeptical of the intelligence of primitive cultures, was nevertheless expecting to be surprised in some way, perhaps by the Jewish influence in this people's history. What we actually saw indeed surprised us, as we came to realize that before us was a people who were not merely ascending a ladder into the modern world but in fact were recovering something they had lost and treasured for thousands of years. For at the origins of their Jewish culture in Ethiopia was a creative explosion of learning and sensibility that is still reflected in their devotion to the Hebrew Bible and its great authors, J and S. This did not help them, of course, with the leather lobby couches, which they piled in a corner, finding it more comfortable to sit on the marble floor.

While at the hotel, we talked to an Ethiopian who was interpreting for the group. What especially shocked Philip Rieff was the ability of these primitive people to not only comprehend his questions about their culture but to actually laugh in response and question him: "Where did this old man come by that hand-carved cane that he was using?" And "What was he writing down in that notebook he carried?" When they were told by the interpreter that Professor Rieff was a world-famous philosopher (*sociologist* didn't translate very well), a young woman of no more than twenty turned to him and asked, "Do you study the Bible?" Professor Rieff hesitated, then said that he regretted not having learned enough Hebrew to do so. It was a startling experience to see Rieff apologize to this young, barefooted African native for his ignorance. She responded to his reply by saying, "I am learning to translate on the computer the Hebrew Bible right here, which I studied in Amharic. My father was also a great philosopher. He held the entire Hebrew Bible, every word of it, in his mind."

So much for "primitive" cultures. As Professor Rieff and I shared a taxi back to our residence as guests of the city of Jerusalem, he reminded me that he had been invited to be the keynote speaker at a conference on the great Hebraic philosopher Martin Buber. He commented, "I don't think the organizers understood how unimpressed I am with the work of Buber, but now I have the feeling that I have come within a heartbeat of meeting a great Jewish philosopher from the lost culture in Ethiopia."

We decided to continue our journey of discovery that day: I invited Rieff to a newly opened Jerusalem restaurant to encounter Yemenite culture for the first time in his life. A young and attractive Yemenite waitress came to our table and began to explain the history and origin of each dish that he inquired about. When she left with our order, we opened the menus out of curiosity. Rieff gasped, for the menu contained pictures of completely naked women interspersed with engravings of saintly Yemenite rabbis. "Now, this is what I call culture shock," he observed.

I understood Professor Rieff to mean that the culture shock experienced by a sophisticated Ivy League professor could still be as strong as that encountered by a native hill-country Ethiopian in modern Jerusalem. For myself, seeing the power of an ancient culture to absorb the latest word in modern thinking—there were computers set up on the lobby floor of the Ethiopian hostel-hotel as well—was breathtaking. And then to see the first signs of creative transformation—the almost avant-garde art of the Yemenite restaurant menu—was a reminder of how exciting the cultural diversity of Solomonic Jerusalem must have been for a writer alive at that time.

Before I left Jerusalem, I met with Ari Rath of the Jerusalem Foundation, who was planning the literary agenda for the three-thousandth birthday of David's Jerusalem, in 1996. Rath asked me if I knew of other American writers who would recognize the significance of this birthday and read from their relevant work. As I pondered this, I realized that once again the most important writers of all were being overlooked. Once more they would be suppressed, even in their own city. Was there any chance that J and S, along with the Solomonic renaissance of writers they represented, would be honored here?

As the question sunk in, I knew that I would be returning to New York that summer of 1992 with a new understanding of the work I would need to do. The original *Book of David* would have been a work that helped transform the city of David into the creative spirit that not only nurtured our major religions, but provided the model for how a great culture rests on the sensibilities of its artists.

In *The Book of J*, I wrote, "For myself as a Jew, the discovery of a unified sensibility and imagination in the J writer reveals hidden strength in our heritage. For a reader unwilling to accept the superhuman author Moses, the humanity of J, her art, offers a fresh, modern midrash." In his work on Genesis for the Anchor Bible in 1964, E. A. Speiser suggested that this would be the task in any recovery of S and his relationship with J. It would require the risk of imaginative thought, one that would honor the risks taken by J and S themselves. Speiser's challenge has been refused for too long. As we complete the celebration of a great cultural city and its founding personality, it seems time to recognize those writers and, in particular, S, who gave us the material for imagining David's singular sensibility—in the form of an individual God, and an individual in his image.

Appendix

SCHOLARS *and*
SOURCES:

*A Critique of the Critics of S,
and a Reply to the Critics of J*

by
Rhonda Rosenberg
with
David Rosenberg

1

In *One Writer's Beginnings* (1984), Eudora Welty remembers, "It had been startling and disappointing to me to find out that story books had been written by *people*, that books were not natural wonders, coming up of themselves like grass." When she writes about the Bible, Welty speaks of it uncomfortably. The subject of where babies come from, which she discusses at length earlier in her book, parallels the subject of where the Bible comes from: It is a problem she failed to solve as a child, though she found a way to manage it, like all of us.

Freud called this question of origins "the oldest and most burning question that assails immature humanity." Our first secrets are sexual. This fact, first explicated by Freud, still provokes dismay and strenuous efforts of suppression in our culture. There continues to be a taboo on our sexual origins, especially as they disturb our notions of childhood. If the undiscoverable origins of babies can be said to be our first intellectual failure as human beings, then the question of the origins of the Bible is certainly our second. The taboo on origins usually prevents most of us from even guessing there are secrets to be discovered about the Bible, or, more precisely, that something was made secret about the Bible and is now lost to our culture.

For Eudora Welty and many of us, the Bible can be revered for the power of its stories. But the pursuit of an understanding about its place in our culture is often interrupted by either a wish for consolation or an ambivalence about "organized religion," as Welty puts it. Although she learns that *people* are implicated in the making of babies just as they are in the making of books, she never even reaches the issue when it comes to the Bible. As a result, she ends up doing something uncharacteristic and fatal to herself as a writer: She resorts to cliché and convention in discussing the work of the Bible.

Welty is certainly not alone. For those who struggle to understand our intellectual failures and the complexity of culture and origins, it is particularly painful to read what continues to be written on the Bible. Consider what W. H. Auden observed about Shakespeare's sonnets, because it applies just as accurately to the poetic writings of J and S:

> Probably, more nonsense has been talked and written, more intellectual and emotional energy expended in vain, on the sonnets of Shakespeare than on any other literary work in the world. Indeed, they have become the best touchstone I know of for distinguishing the sheep from the goats, those, that is, who love poetry for its own sake and understand its nature, from those who only value poems either as historical documents or because they express feelings or beliefs of which the reader happens to approve.

This appendix is about distinguishing "the sheep from the goats" when it comes to the Bible. As we shall see, our sheep are those who have made themselves vulnerable to the original sensibilities behind the work of the Bible, particularly in what has come to be known to us as the court history and the Yahwist narrative. The goats are those who have resisted, in one way or another, the original authors and the culture they inhabited. This appendix is about the many forms of this resistance and what it blinds us to in the Bible and in our own culture.

However much Eudora Welty fails us on the subject of the Bible, she nonetheless shows where to begin and who to look to as a guide. We begin with "beginnings," with origins. And we look to those who have made the problem of origins their life's work, either in science, criticism, or literature and art. I began with Ms. Welty because she herself began with origins and the taboos we place on them. And not surprisingly, I found myself going from her to Sigmund Freud in trying to establish a framework for interrogating the avoidance of origins in the scholarship of those we have come to rely upon as authorities on reading the Bible.

It was in *The Interpretation of Dreams* that I found my model. Freud begins with an account of earlier writers on the subject of dreams that carries him into a demonstration of his own view and method. His critique forms the context for an argument—"that dreams are capable of interpretation." This was quite a thing to push for at the time, since the scholarly consensus was that there was little that was meaningful or knowable in dreams, which were basically considered products of a somatic process. But what was no doubt even more unusual was the careful attention Freud directed to lay opinion and the conceptions of dreams held by primitive and classical cultures. Where most scholars would have been afraid to linger too long over the beliefs and probings of the prescientific world, Freud felt that there was something that could not be ignored or dismissed in the attention paid by the ancients to dreams, no matter how conflated with superstitious thinking. What mattered to Freud is what matters to readers of David, who want to understand the context of a Hebraic culture with roots in prehistory. Freud wanted us to take notice that in prehistory, dreams represented a problem of meaning and interpretation: "I have been forced to perceive that here, once more, we have one of those not infrequent cases where an

ancient and stubbornly retained popular belief seems to have come
nearer to the truth of the matter than the opinion of modern science."
Freud alerts us that dreams possessed an importance to aboriginal cultures in knowing themselves as a species. Dreams informed their poetry,
which influenced David to transform shaman songs into psalms, and
influenced S to create a poetic realism rooted in an indigenous sense of
interior life.

This is our project as well in *The Book of David*. And where Freud is
concerned with the subject of "the dream-problem" and "the problem of
dream-interpretation" in the scholarship of his peers, we are interested
in what could be called the *author-problem* and the intellectual failure on
the part of our best-known scholars and critics to confront the original
authors of the Bible and the culture they created. Like Freud, I confess
that I have been forced to recognize that popular and ancestral opinion
offers more insight into "the truth of the matter" than disquisitions of
many of our scholarly experts. How can I possibly say such a thing, particularly after all the centuries of effort to break through superstitious
tradition on the subject of divine authorship and inspiration? Why
would I prefer notions of an old man in the sky and the "Five Books of
Moses" to images of a scribal school or a great redactor tradition that
compiled and recomposed the text? Because in such notions we can see,
so clearly and bitterly sweet, a wish displaced, a problem attempted but
failing to be solved. And in a way, the closer we are to seeing this, the
closer we are to the original authors.

Let me try to explain. Great writers play with the wishes and problems of the human psyche and those of the culture of which they are a
part. There is nothing extraordinary in such an observation, but it is one
often overlooked and, I would say, deliberately obscured by many contemporary scholars of the Bible. Why is it so hard for us to take in a
great author? Postmodern criticism is often characterized as a killing off
of the singularity of authorship. The work of the postmodern critic
Jacques Derrida is usually held up in accusation and disdain on this

point, but I find it interesting that the disclaimers are almost always the disposers of authorship. Derrida himself is hardly a disposer, choosing to linger in the singularity of an author. It is ironic that I became a reader of Derrida's on account of those unable to read an author, particularly a biblical one. And though I am unsure yet how close Derrida comes to understanding the author-problem, what matters is that he grapples with it, and it is that grappling that is woefully missing in the scrutinies of most of our contemporary experts on the Bible.

At a certain point, I found myself foraging the bookshelves for translations of great ancient writers. What I wanted to read in particular were the introductory commentaries and notes on translation. I would mention only one of my findings now—Bernard Knox's introduction to a translation of Homer's *The Iliad* (1991) by Robert Fagles. What stands out in Knox's retrospective of scholarly preoccupations is the question of what kind of author Homer was. Was he a Shakespeare or Milton, or a great bard or balladeer who, at most, inspired some later scholar to put together and redact what we now take to be *The Iliad*? The parallel to trends in scholarly thinking about the origins of the great biblical narratives was striking. But what I now see as most striking about Knox's retrospective is how he reveals a struggle, a tug-of-war between the scholars who would possess the text and a powerful author who cannot be pried loose of it, no matter how dead or lost he is to us.

It is stunning to read the translator's preface and realize how Robert Fagles misses what Knox is after, assuming the estimations of Homer were the point of the essay. Knox may have been assigned the task of providing a scholarly, grounded characterization of Homer. But what he ends up doing is telling a story of his own, that of "a great poet" who "marshaled the resources of an age-old traditional art to create something new." It is *The Iliad*'s author who is the hero of Knox's story, not its scholars. And in this, Knox takes a risk that many of our expert readers of the Bible fail to take. It is an intellectual risk that strives to honor the risk taken by great authors such as Homer, Shakespeare, J, and S. It is foremost a risk of vulnerability, of holding one's ground in the midst of a great author, a strong reader of culture and human sensibility.

For many centuries Moses was considered the hero of the Pentateuch, God's scribe, the author of the Bible's first five books. We have gone from myth to theory, from what Freud called notions of "the great man" to the neutered images of great redactors and objectifications called composite texts. Gone are a people's love objects, the idealized personalities of a Moses with a staff or a Yahweh taking an evening walk in the Garden of Eden. And in our detachment from these objects, we have lost sight of the basic problems that the efforts of culture attempt to solve. And we have lost touch with the human, sexualized basis of culture, particularly those fully sexual individuals who give us a vital culture and keep it alive through artistic commentary and restoration.

Freud was very clear in his mind on the myth of Moses, both as a leader and an author; however, he knew that it was only through Moses—a people's idealization—that he could begin to clarify the basis of a culture. He attended to this particular personality not only in his *Moses and Monotheism* but also in "The Moses of Michelangelo," in which we see how Moses becomes a figure, that is, a sensibility at the hands of another sensibility—an artist. But who is to help us with the figure of Yahweh in Genesis, who appears as the biggest, most complex sensibility in the Bible? J could help us, but for most of our scholars there can be no help from J. And who is to help us with the figure of David in 2 Samuel? Again, we could be helped by an author called S, the Court Historian. But instead, we are led away from S to another idealized object, one heavily invested in by the "goats" among our scholars—the redactor or the community of redactors.

In his part of the commentary to *The Book of J*, Harold Bloom referred to J as a fiction. But those like Robert Alter, who later judged this to be a sensible acknowledgment, completely missed the point. Alter criticized Bloom for letting J take on such a "definite" shape, in other words, for becoming so alive, such a "historical figure." But with that observation, Alter had penned himself with the goats, with those disabled from understanding the nature of literature and what constitutes its special facticity. What does it mean when the heads of our scholars hurt with the fullness of a literary figure or a historical fiction?

For a short interlude after the publication of *The Book of J*, it was the biblical scholars who were squeezed and pressed, not the Bible's original authors. And in that opening of time, a great literary work came alive and the sensibility behind it was given expression. A literary fiction became more real than a scholarly fiction, a literary author more real than a literary editor. And what was compressed in our scholars was fully revealed—the faculty of imagination. The literary sensibility of J and the literary imagination of *The Book of J* made the heads of scholars hurt because it asked of them what they could not give and what they would prefer to keep pressed down in the rest of us, that is, imagination and a vulnerability to (as opposed to critical distance from) literary experience.

2

Apologies, Apologies

A standard reference for many of us wishing to know more is the Anchor Bible series. In 1984 it issued a new translation of 2 Samuel by P. Kyle McCarter. What concerns us here is McCarter's introduction, particularly the section on narrative sources. Having fulfilled the obligation of laying out the Deuteronomistic editorial structure—the redactor—McCarter contrasts his position to that of Carlson or the school of Uppsala scholarship, which believes that it is virtually impossible to determine anything beyond or behind the edited form of what is referred to as an "epic." This reference to 2 Samuel as an epic helps McCarter appear open and attuned to cultural resources. However, the invocation of the epic form is characteristic of those who avoid authorship and forewarns us that this scholar is about to enwrap himself in the security blanket of narrative. By the time he is through, narrative shall be indistinguishable from an obelisk.

McCarter believes that "ancient written documents lie behind many parts of the book," suggested by parallels to ancient Near Eastern literature. Moreover, he dates the story of Abishalom's (Absalom's) revolt to the time of David. When he takes up what he subtitles the "Succession Narrative Hypothesis," he states that the "dominant composition from a narrative point of view is the story of Abishalom's revolt." He lays out the dimensions of the narrative, referring to all the proper sources of thought. Chapters 13 through 20 appear to be the core, while other scholars like Roth extend it to include 1 Kings 1 and 2, which describe the rise of Solomon. McCarter defines it as follows: "This old narrative was composed in the time of Solomon by a supporter of the king."

McCarter summarizes the motivation and plot devised by this individual and then proceeds to a commentary that describes the narrative as a historiographical document. His intention is to review the field's literature of supposition about the identity and intention of the writer of this narrative strand. We will see, though, that the concepts of identity and intention are confronted in institutional terms. Also, institutions are portrayed with a fairly parochial and unimaginative framework, with little indication of a conception of the life or culture of the time—even as the subject of this narrative is the life of David and the culture in which he lived. It is not coincidental that McCarter cannot undertake the succession narrative except as a hypothesis, turning the methodology of science into intellectual constraint. In fact McCarter uses the tenets of science out of context, because he uses them as a cover.

As McCarter continues with his scholarly obligation to report the literature on the nature of this source, hypothesis becomes a corset to hide the discomforting presence of what he himself recognizes, at least in Chapters 13 through 20, as a "tightly knit account." Such a phenomenon, to carry out his science metaphor, suggests that there must be a single writer. And it's interesting that McCarter uses the term "writer" most of the time. "Author" would be too much to bear because it would suggest a creative mind, which would place McCarter in what he obviously sees as hostile territory: authorship and subjectivity as opposed to narrative constructions and objective material; reading and critique as opposed to excavation. For to come up against an author is to come up against an intellectual force or, as Foucault put it in *What Is an Author?* a "founder[s] of discursivity," someone who has produced not just their own work but has defined the possibilities and the rules of what constitutes a text.

S's narrative as a hypothesis is attributed by McCarter to Rost, who is understood in von Rad's interpretation. Von Rad approaches the narrative as an "epoch-making historiographical achievement by a writer who is notable for 'his habitual restraint,'" which nonetheless permits personal viewpoint and a "strong theological undercurrent." As McCarter interprets von Rad, "a theological interpretation is successfully introduced into the narrative without compromising the remarkable secularity of plot and character that distinguishes the whole. The result is a 'wholly new conception of the nature of God's activity in history.'" Having set his context—the narrative as historiography, or history writing—McCarter summons what he believes to be an opposing view in the form of Whybray, who characterizes the narrative as a "novel," emphasizing its "high literary quality" over its historical theme.

But Whybray does not rest with this characterization; in fact, he pursues Rost's theme of the narrative's function as political propaganda. This offers Whybray a tie-in for his thesis that the narrative fits under the influence of wisdom literature and that furthermore, the author "was not merely a man who shared the general outlook of the wisdom teachers, but was himself a wisdom teacher in the sense that he set out deliberately to illustrate specific proverbial teaching for the benefit of the pupils and ex-pupils of the schools." Now, McCarter does not like Whybray's ideas about the narrative as wisdom literature, but he does find himself supporting the thesis of political propaganda, which he states is best drawn out by Thornton, who defines the narrative as answering this question: Why Solomon? (rather than the question Rost imagined, Who will succeed David?).

We now come to the origin of the "succession narrative"—as S's book is sometimes called—and its terminology. The narrative is seen to answer a political, institutional question. McCarter's term for it is the Solomonic Apology, the narrative as "court apologetic." This kind of interpretation goes along with his diminutive conception of culture and institutions, committing the intellectual mistake that Lionel Trilling defined and elucidated so well in his cultural critique "Freud and the Crisis in Our Culture." That mistake is to read culture through the idea of "man-in-community" or, rather, to base one's understanding of culture on the concept (and one might say the wish fulfillment) of civilization. This mistake carries McCarter so far as to imagine (to the extent that he does) that the author of the narrative is performing an apologia for the new political institution inaugurated by David, as well as for David himself as a symbol of civilization. It is also worth noting that McCarter speaks in terms of "a work of court apologetic," unable to even use the noun form of the word—"apologist"—which would suggest a human being.

While McCarter embraces the idea of the narrative as court apologetic, he does not embrace the implication, that it is "the original and unified composition of a Solomonic writer." This is less an issue of what period the writer of this narrative belonged to than it is an issue of a single author writing an original, creative work. McCarter goes on to tease out the various narratives of 2 Samuel with particular attention to their relationship to 1 Kings 1–2. He estimates that 2 Samuel is comprised of three "discrete compositions": 1) the story of David's rise to power, 2) the story of Abishalom's revolt, and 3) the story of the Gibeonites' revenge and David's patronage of Merribbaal. He notes the "self-contained character" of the story of Abishalom's revolt, casting it into a public versus private scheme: "The account shows the private issues that precipitated the public events of the revolt. The narrator's purpose is to elicit sympathy for David in the aftermath of the crisis."

McCarter's position is that only 1 Kings 1–2 can be counted as part of the succession narrative. This leads him into the controversy among scholars over whether the narrative had been originally anti-Solomonic or anti-Davidic, that is, if what we now read reflects a redaction, and that the tension in the narrative indicates redaction. McCarter rejects this interpretation, defining this tension as an inherent characteristic of the literary form of royal apology or apologetic writing: "Apologetic writing presents unfavorable circumstances forthrightly in order to cast a favorable light on them by a variety of literary means. By its very nature, then, it holds conflicting ideas in literary tension. The elimination of the literary blandishments of the author by appeal to higher critical or other considerations, therefore, will inevitably produce a recital of unfavorable circumstances, but it will also distort the writer's intended product beyond recovery. It is a mistake to rely heavily on the criterion of narrative tension for identifying redactional material in these stories, when such tension is the very essence of the writer's technique." The reader leaps for the liberation McCarter offers in the form of the public versus private, pro versus con debate. Here is something that seems to bring us closer to an imaginative, complex sensibility as we confront this "narrative tension."

However, McCarter brings it up in order to continue the delineation of a narrative, not a sensibility. He seems barely to hang on to the threads of tension, never managing to follow the weave into what E. A. Speiser in the Anchor Bible promises: "Its object is to make the Bible accessible to the modern reader; its method is to arrive at the meaning . . . , and to reconstruct the ancient setting of the biblical story, as well as the circumstances of its transcription and the characteristics of its transcribers." The tension for McCarter is merely that of the public sphere: private issues colliding with public obligations, whether the writer is pro- or anti-David. Or, it is the kingship, the political institution. To read the court history in this way is like reading the celebrated *New Yorker* essays by Harold Brodkey on his infection with HIV for what it has to say about the politics of AIDS—instead of as a profoundly human document.

One reads Brodkey to read a literary author, which we are tipped off to in his title, "To My Readers." It could also be said that Brodkey plays with the same literary form that occupies McCarter: the apologetic. And it suggests that if Brodkey is playing with this form, what might S have been playing with? We will never learn this from McCarter, because once he can locate the tension in a literary form, he is protected from the terrain of play that defines authorship and separates it from the academic mind-set.

McCarter does offer a short paragraph on the "literary considerations" of 2 Samuel, as if an afterthought. In his preference for Conroy's effort to give us "a fuller appreciation of its nature as a story," McCarter pretends to reveal what a literary approach to the Bible is all about: the Bible as great storytelling. This has been the path taken to diminish other great works of culture. Storytelling is associated with the primitive and coincides with the oral view of the Bible. By focusing on storytelling, one avoids authorship and the idea that the reader is reading more than a story, that he or she is also reading an author.

In McCarter's notes on the Bathsheba affair, he tries to account for the beginning: "When the time of year at which the kings had marched out came around again . . ." Then he tries to account for why David stayed behind. McCarter's note on this is a pointed illustration of his approach to the succession narrative and to literature, authorship, and translation in general. As always, he must nail these things down as quickly as possible. As he tries to account for "return of the year, at the time of," he aptly lays out his resources and parallels to other parts of the Bible, trying to find out when that time of the year is, or what it is. He finally decides that "this probably was, as a matter of fact, spring, the time for war and love; but our text does not say so." Yet it never occurs to McCarter that the time of the year, time of the month, is a recurrent theme or play on words, and that S may in fact be playing with the *convention* of spring being the time for war and love.

McCarter strives to show how the narrative fails to exonerate David for not going with the army. Yet one of the first things that strikes you about this early chapter in S's narrative is how different it is from others that preceded it in the books of Samuel, namely those written by other writers. Here we see David awaking, perhaps not able to sleep, taking a contemplative walk on the roof, and spotting a woman—not merely spotting a woman, but a knockout. Here is the foundation for most Hollywood romantic comedies: Man, left alone, comes up against beautiful woman, etc. It reminds one of *The Seven Year Itch* with Tom Ewell and Marilyn Monroe. Of course, it would take the whole movie to get to where this chapter arrives in one paragraph, namely, the two of them in bed (not to mention the woman getting pregnant). Meanwhile, it is very comic to see David trying to get Uriah over to Bathsheba, to sleep with her and cover the pregnancy. But Uriah is so, so, so Davidic—he won't sleep with her. One could say he's really asking for it. And he gets it.

McCarter notes that when David tells Uriah to go down to his house and wash his feet, this may mean no more than "refresh yourself," although when feet come up in other parts of the Bible, as in Ruth, it is as a suggestive euphemism for sexual intercourse. McCarter seems to miss how funny this is: David telling Uriah to go wash his feet and then asking, "Why didn't you go down to your house?" And then McCarter notes that it is ironic that Uriah delivers his own death warrant. But as always, McCarter must nail it down with parallels to literary forms, this time in *The Iliad*, describing it as a "motif, widespread in world literature, of the messenger carrying his own death warrant." But can one help reading this passage without thinking of W. C. Fields playing the king of Klopstokia in the classic movie *Million Dollar Legs?* "Send Uriah where there is hard fighting, then withdraw from him, so that he will be struck down and die." Rather than S being sarcastic here or trying to catch David in hypocrisy or sin, he is as deadpan as can be.

One way McCarter tries to account for David's behavior is to characterize it as a midlife crisis. "David's misconduct is presented bluntly and without explanation," he writes, "as if any hint of his motivation might mitigate his crime in the mind of the reader." Then McCarter contrasts this to earlier accounts in Samuel, not even bothering to note or remember that they were not written by S. The effort is to show that David's behavior is presented "without a word of mitigation." Based on this, he wants to demonstrate that the writer of 2 Samuel 11–12 "is another contribution from the prophetic hand that introduced, for example, the report of Saul's Amalekite campaign in 1 Samuel 15, where the king commits a crime, comes under prophetic censure, and confesses." McCarter describes this prophetic writer's technique as editorial.

All of this is introduced with the claim, "It is extraordinary, therefore, that a majority of modern scholars have followed Rost in thinking of chaps. 11–12 as an original part of a document also including chaps. 13–20. Can the narrator who describes David's cold contrivance of the murder of the steadfast and blameless Uriah be the narrator who takes such pains to show David's innocence in the death of the rebel Abishalom?" It is important to note the framework of interpretation here, which is one of morality. The interpreter's effort is to find a place for David's guilt or innocence, to find his exoneration or lack thereof in the narrative—or, as McCarter also deigns to say, the narrator. McCarter notes that David's affair or behavior is "presented bluntly," and he supplies what he thinks is a complementary translation, equivalent to a writer just reporting the facts, where what counts is the moral tally. And since it stacks up against David in McCarter's view, the narrator can report the facts only because he has to, or is forced to, because David's behavior cannot be glossed over.

But is S really the flat-footed journalist McCarter describes, or is he a creative, intelligent author? And is the S narrative blunt journalistic reporting or a partly deadpan creation by an author who knows exactly what he is doing and who or what he is doing it for? It certainly isn't for a moral tally or to provide a historical exoneration or a straightforward account for history or God or God's people. Rather, it is for—as Trilling put it—an "effort of culture." Not for or by culture, but for and by a creative sensibility.

Genre

A common preoccupation of biblical scholars concerned with the court history is how to define its nature or its genre and purpose. To understand how this problem becomes a problem and how it gets worked out, it is useful to examine A. A. Anderson's introduction to his translation of 2 Samuel for the *Word Biblical Commentary* (1989). Attempting a characterization, Anderson states that "there is no need to reject those views which assert that the SN [succession narrative] is a real work of art . . . although we would doubt this was the primary purpose in the composition of the SN." He makes this statement after considering the succession narrative as apology—a literary type—and as "simply political propaganda." Of these, Anderson prefers the characterization of apology over propaganda, arguing that it captures more complexity of purpose while keeping in mind the narrative's quality of being basically "an 'official' interpretation of significant events." He feels that perhaps it can be described as historical narrative, but only loosely, maintaining that "it is doubtful that it was ever intended as a work of history approaching our sense of the word."

So it is not unexpected to find Anderson unable to pursue the narrative as art, even though he does not discount it. Yet as he resolves not to discount it, he nonetheless makes it irrelevant. The art of the succession narrative is subsumed under a literary form where authorship is transformed into apologetics. With a court apologist, Anderson can avoid a sensibility with imaginative purposes, using a subject rather than being used by it. Thus, we begin to see what is behind the preoccupation with genre and purposes: an anxiety over being in the midst of a strong author. The nature of the court history becomes a problem because the author-problem cannot be confronted—much less resolved.

Yet Anderson's aim appears to be to make the text more accessible to the general reader. In many respects the *Word Biblical Commentary*, both in print and approach, is more approachable than the Anchor Bible version. But like McCarter, Anderson is beset by intellectual anxieties which he has no compunction in passing on to the layman. As is incumbent on the scholar or academic, Anderson preoccupies himself with defining the succession narrative, just as McCarter does. But Anderson is particularly intense in what he refers to as "the quest for the beginning of the SN." He even puts "beginning" in italics and states: "Chapter 9 has often been taken as the start of the narrative; however, it opens with the words, 'Is there still anyone left of the house of Saul?' which provides a hardly satisfactory opening of the SN."

Professor Anderson then proceeds to construct what he considers is a better, more sensible, and more meaningful beginning out of verses from earlier chapters as well as later ones. We must ask: Why the labor? Why can there not be something missing, at the very least? Why does the speculative search for narrative logic and motivation overshadow all other speculations and considerations, not least of which is imagining an author and a culture? Anderson does broach the identity of the author toward the end of his introduction: "The identity of the author of the SN remains an insoluble problem. Any proposed identifications, such as Ahimaaz son of Zadok, or Nathan the prophet, or an unnamed royal tutor or scribe, are merely informed guesswork. However, we can agree with Jones that 'it can be reasonably claimed that the work originated from court circles.'" To even come close to this subject of an author causes Anderson to perform as a reporter, careful to deliver the news in quotes. It is disturbing to observe the same obsessions operating in both Anderson and McCarter: the retreat to apologia and the scrutiny of the narrative as political propaganda. Neither is really interested in politics. Both are absorbed in accounting for character and purpose, particularly David's, and the hard-to-get-to-know scribe that put the narrative together. Examples are marshaled to show S's narrative as apology but none are presented to portray a dynamic person behind the narrative.

So, the question arises, why are our contemporary biblical scholars afraid to read S's court history as an imaginative work? Once again, the answer is the taboo on authorship. In other words, a great writer who also happened to be Jewish would upset the scholarly applecart.

4

The Hand Behind the Work

When scholars do undertake authorship as a primary focus, it is usually presented as an archaeological problem to be sifted through or a puzzle to be solved. One such book still in print was published in the 1980s by Richard Friedman. Its title is meant to be seductive: *Who Wrote the Bible?* Its cover advertises that "for centuries scholars have assembled small pieces of an enormous puzzle. Now modern research and recent archaeological discoveries offer answers to the mystery of who wrote the Bible." The reader is invited to an answer, properly grounded in scientific sifting. One appeal is surely the love of a good mystery; it can be scary and upending, but there is always an answer in the end.

Yet Friedman's brand of answers conspires to relieve the reader from the responsibility to think—and, most of all, even to imagine. His answers perpetuate a deep cultural confusion about the nature of science and the analytical task. Far from offering resolution, Friedman's enterprise is one of further mystification and dullness. Still, it is disturbing to recognize one's own susceptibility to the Friedman mystique, and it should therefore be instructive to understand it in pursuing the problem before us. It is a problem not unrelated to archaeology, and Friedman turns to that discipline in his effort to solve it or be inside it and take the reader with him. What that problem is can best be understood by probing this effort to be "inside."

Opening with a paragraph that reviews the Bible's singular importance in Western culture, Friedman offers the reasons it is so important: It is the most quoted, translated, studied, and most often purchased book. Further, "People have lived by it and died for it. And we do not know who wrote it." It is easy to overlook the obfuscation in this initial statement of facticity about authorship. After all, Friedman seems to be asking all the right questions: "If we think that the Bible is a great work of literature, then who were the artists? If we encounter an author when we read a work, to whatever degree and be it fiction or nonfiction, then whom do we encounter when we read the Bible?" Moreover, he seems to confront how the issue of authorship emerged and proceeded in a section entitled "Six Hundred Years of Investigation." The reader looking for reference to Spinoza will find it, along with a number of other names associated with questioning of authority and traditional readings of the Bible. Granted, the reference to Spinoza is slight, confined to his refutation of Moses as the author of the Pentateuch. But after all, this is not a book about Spinoza.

Yet, upon reflection, it is interesting to consider what Friedman does not quote from in Spinoza's work. In the preface to *A Theologico-Political Treatise*, Spinoza begins by setting terms of argument directly opposite to what Friedman presses forward as the frame for investigating biblical authorship. Spinoza writes, "Men would never be superstitious, if they could govern all their circumstances by set rules, or if they were always favoured by fortune: but being frequently driven into straits where rules are useless, and being often kept fluctuating pitiably between hope and fear by the uncertainty of fortune's greedily coveted favours, they are consequently, for the most part, very prone to credulity." And most men, Spinoza continues, "never display less scruple or more zeal than when they are interpreting Scripture." It is clear that Spinoza's interrogation was motivated by something much deeper than the issue of Mosaic authorship. But Friedman tells us on the first page of his introduction that such investigations into authorship "did not develop as a controversy of religion versus science or religion versus the secular." Perhaps even this statement may pass by and not seem disingenuous at first. Perhaps Friedman intended it as a way to avoid alienating certain readers. But I do not think so. I think it is symptomatic of an effort of suppression running insidiously throughout Friedman's book.

Strong words? Yet I am propelled forward by remembering what Spinoza was trying to recover with his biblical investigations and what Friedman works *against* recovering with his "synthesis." Spinoza was after more than a refutation of Moses as Pentateuchal author. He was trying to recover a lost and suppressed culture and history by confronting the issue of authorship. Moreover, he was trying to map the analytical task and a terrain of critique. That's why, centuries later, he remains an intellectual resource for scientists of interpretation and analysis, such as Sigmund Freud. Spinoza's ambitions, however, are antithetical to those found in *Who Wrote the Bible?* Ostensibly, Friedman's ambition is to deliver the authors of the Bible to the reader. Yet, in presenting his hypothesis of authorship, the reader is introduced to J as well as E, P, and D as "documents" and "sources," not authors.

Let us imagine that this can be explained as good scholarship. Friedman appears to be carefully marking and acknowledging the tradition of source criticism, particularly the work of Wellhausen. This permits him to then talk about what his own contribution will be, how it will fit in, and how he will "be more specific about who the writers of the Bible were: not only when they lived, but where they resided . . . whom they liked, whom they opposed, and their political and religious purposes in writing their works." He also promises that he will give us a picture of the biblical world that produced these authors and their texts. Instead of a picture, however, Friedman wants to deliver answers and, more important, a standardization of answering. Since I'm not averse to answers, I readily followed Friedman into his biblical world—but it spoke only of how the *people lived*. I did not find a culture or a context for authorship. Instead, I found traits of a people, laid out much like excavated bones, labeled and classified. The bones of the culture were tagged with the term "people": "The people of Israel spoke Hebrew. Other languages of the area were similar to Hebrew: Phoenician, Canaanite (Ugaritic), Aramaic, and Moabite are all in the Semitic family of languages. . . . People wrote documents on papyrus and sealed them with stamps pressed in wet clay. . . . People lived in one- and two-story homes. . . . People ate beef, lamb. . . . They made wine . . . pots and jars.

I continued to hope there would be more as we got into the twelfth century B.C., when, as Friedman explained, there was more historical information on which to reconstruct a picture of the setting of the authors. Although I thought I was above this plodding dullness, I had already been caught by it. I almost called it an ordinary dullness, but that would underestimate its pathology and abort further investigation. It is a pathology that confines intellectual effort to a laying out of our cultural bones—never getting to the meat, the nutrient sources of what makes a culture. Friedman's kind of dullness erases efforts of culture. Lionel Trilling, for one, was a student of this dullness and its pathological effect on our culture. He wrote about the pathology of reading culture through ideas of community and the consequent expelling of sensibility and imagination. What we find in Friedman is a constant need to expel the culture and the original authors of the Bible.

What does it mean to talk about great writing in terms of what is in it and who wrote it? Friedman's premise, that he will tell us about who wrote the Bible, turns out to mean that he will inventory the story elements of such sources as J and then follow clues about the identities of the authors in terms of where they came from and what their politics were. He states that biblical detectives "were able to identify at least four hands writing in the first five books of the Bible" and that "there was the hand of an extremely skillful collector known as a redactor." This recounting and how it is stated by Friedman foreshadows a deep aversion to ever seeing more than the hands of the writers in his book. He delivers these hands much like an ivory hunter delivers the tusks of an elephant, never imagining the intelligence and evolutionary narrative lost and erased. And what is lost to the reader as a consequence is the hand at work, that is, the sensibility and cultural narrative behind the writing.

How would we react to someone holding forth on why *Hamlet* was written or the facts on file about where Shakespeare lived in Elizabethan England? Knowing that such things have been taken care of by the *Encyclopaedia Brittanica* should make one secure enough to venture further into *Hamlet* as great writing, to confront its author as a compelling intelligence, a powerful reader and critic of culture. But Friedman robs us of such an opportunity with the Bible: "There is still much to be discovered about who wrote J and E. We do not know the precise dates when they lived, and we do not know their names. I think that what we do know is more important. We know something about their world and about how that world produced these stories that still delight and teach us. Still, we may be dissatisfied until we can be more specific about the writers. So let me turn to source D. We can know even more about the person who assembled it than about those who wrote J and E—perhaps even his name." The pathology in this passage of Friedman's can begin to be understood if we consider what it would mean to talk about *The Odyssey* in terms of the editors and translators that have arranged or set the text. Going inside the Bible without J is like going inside *The Odyssey* without Homer.

The consequences go beyond the category of an unsolved mystery or an incomplete archaeological record. For Friedman, J is never more than a source or document that had a writer, possibly female, from the Judean court, who probably wrote sometime before 722 B.C. He anchors this person in a "world" rather than a culture because to do more would raise the writer too far above anonymity and too close in status to the redactor D—whom Friedman can barely wait to embrace after filing the facts on J. To pull oneself back from the brink of this nightmarish vision of literature, it helps to quickly read a note from an editor or translator of Greek, such as William Arrowsmith's foreword to W. S. Merwin's translation of *Iphigenia at Aulis* by Euripides. In Arrowsmith's words, we are reminded that an author can be thought to possess a text and confront a culture in the process: "Nowhere is scholarly timidity more evident than when the scholar is dealing with a dubious text, its pages studded with obelisks and emendations. And the corruption of the text of this play . . . has meant . . . that the play has been treated with gingerly and, at best, very lukewarm enthusiasm. A pity, because even in its mutilated shape the *Iphigenia at Aulis* is clearly one of Euripides' most searching critiques of the malaise of Greek culture and politics at the close of the fifth century. The play dramatizes what has been lost, by juxtaposing memory with reality, then recreating the real as something not simply derived from an unrecapturable heroic past, but constantly recreated."

Oh, to read something like that in Friedman. But it is not to be because Friedman's authors are facts on file, anonymous bones to be tagged and shelved away as quickly as possible. There is no sense of J as an intelligent sensibility creating a work that engaged the inventions and losses of a culture. Nor is there any sense of the possibility of a sophisticated and complex culture in which there was something that could already be lost, inviting restoration and reworking by an author or artist of the caliber of Shakespeare, Homer, or Euripides.

What would it mean to see the hand behind the work? A simple but powerful example of what is needed and what is greviously missing in Friedman is Frank O'Hara's classic essay of art criticism, entitled "Porter Paints a Picture." It is interesting to note that O'Hara begins by telling us where Fairfield Porter lived. He even describes the house in which Porter lived. Rather than filing Porter away, this attention to physical setting, and then biography and physical appearance, becomes a mirror of Porter's attention to a canvas, or what O'Hara defines as composition. Moreover, it is the beginning of the formulation of a sensibility. O'Hara's task will be to match the consciousness of composition which he traces in Porter. To do this, he must carefully detail and interpret what he calls the "conscious procedure" in Porter's work of painting the "Portrait of

Katharine." And he must imagine a sensibility, for as he explains, "Composition is a function of the sensibility; it is the personal statement of the insight which observation and insight afford."

This is what is missing in Friedman's answers on who wrote the Bible. As O'Hara's essay makes very clear, the aim is not to deliver answers but to imagine the working out of a composition and the sensibility behind that work. This is both an interpretive and analytical task. It requires an understanding of consciousness and the will to interpret it. Moreover, it demands knowledge of the unconscious, in both its cultural and psychological manifestations—that there is a childhood of culture as well as of human beings, that the problem always trying to be solved, especially in great writing, is one of origins. At the center of the problem of origins is loss. How we have constructed ourselves and our culture is often lost to us. To grow, to recreate, we must restore to consciousness those constructions, those origins of agency. That is the basic problem that every great writer must face and make his or her own. But it is a problem that Friedman is incapable of making his own. Instead of contributing to the work of restoration as he promises with his title, he buries what has been lost deeper with every chapter. Most important, he obscures the nature of the task required in recovering who wrote the Bible.

Even as Friedman tries to take in the original authors or what he would feel more comfortable in calling the writers of the original sources, there is an undoing, an underlying need to get rid of or expel authorship and culture. This becomes painfully evident when he attempts to discuss the court history of David. We first encounter mention of the court history as Friedman is putting together his picture of the "world that produced the Bible." We learn about David and his empire and the large amount of source material, including "a lengthy text known as the Court History of David," which Friedman describes as "a work which is both beautifully written and a remarkable example of history-writing, remarkable because it openly criticizes its heroes."

The remaining references to the court history are contained mostly within a discussion of the Deuteronomic historian, who, more than anyone else in Friedman's book, takes on shape and power.

We are introduced to Martin Noth, the biblical scholar who teased out a strong connection between Deuteronomy and the subsequent six books of the Bible, which includes 2 Samuel and the court history. As Friedman recounts, Noth demonstrated that these writings were "a thoughtfully arranged work": "It told a continuous story, a flowing account of the history of the people of Israel in their land. It was not by one author. It contained various sections, written by various people (such as the court history of David, and the stories of Samuel). The finished product, nonetheless, was the work of one person." In Friedman's description of this person, we finally see a hand at work, selecting, editing, and arranging texts.

As the assembler of the stories of the Early Prophets, this person emerges as probably our most preeminent scholar and editor, responsible for what Friedman terms "The Creation of the Deuteronomistic History." This is the first time any part of the Bible is referred to as a "creation" by Friedman. We are told that the Deuteronomistic historian "took texts" containing the stories of Joshua and Jericho, "added a few lines at the beginning and at the end to set the story in a certain light," thus giving us the Book of Joshua. He took the texts telling of Deborah, Gideon, and Samson and gave us the Book of Judges. Friedman then explains the making of 1 and 2 Samuel: "Next he placed the stories of Samuel at Shiloh: the stories of Saul and of David, the first kings. This became the book of 1 Samuel. After that he set the Court History of David. That became the book of 2 Samuel." That's it, that is the very last that we hear of the court history, and it is not accidental that we hear it in terms of "took," "set," and "placed." Friedman is more comfortable with the taking, placing, and setting of texts by the D historian than he is with the author of the court history. In fact, he cannot even bring himself to once acknowledge an original author in connection with this narrative.

Most critics agree that the author of S's narrative is the finest prose writer in the Bible. Yet, Friedman basically ignores this writer and barely mentions the narrative. Would we be satisfied with a scholar or critic that referred to a Shakespearean play as "beautifully written" or "a remarkable example of history-writing"? Is the court history "remarkable because it openly criticizes its heroes"? But having paid his compliments, Friedman can then file this narrative and its author away under "court history" and get on with the really important work of D and the taking of texts. Also filed away is David and along with him another opportunity to discuss a singular culture. David is filed away under popular headings of "well-known hero" and "major figure" as well as such academic ones as statecraft, empire-building, and power struggle—king versus priest, king versus king. In Friedman's hands, Davidic culture is reduced to talk of family dynasties, military history, and political geography. Without an author and without a culture, we are limited to a political atlas, tracing the rise and fall of an empire, the movements of tribes, the location of capitals. What is lost to us are the original authors and the culture they lived in, critiqued, and even reimagined. But then there is no place for imagination or any other effort of culture on Friedman's map of the Bible and its writers.

It is hard to accept this absence of interest in ancient Hebraic culture and the great writers of the biblical narratives in such a book as Friedman's. And it is difficult to witness the degeneration of scholarship, as we see Friedman burrowing into the source history, using it to blind us from the original authors. Should we be surprised at what happens to J? When it comes to the first author of the Pentateuch, the great originator of biblical writing, we find a writer reduced to caricature. Yet Friedman seems to care about the biblical text. He has devoted his professional life to it. So it is all the more tragic when we consider how

Friedman uses the text as a screen to hide behind. It is as if the entire Jewish biblical tradition consisted of writers who were concubines, hidden behind the screen of the text. We must face what Friedman cannot and tries his hardest to suppress. Without culture, the text is a mere skeleton of dry speculations advanced by upholders of a convention that tells us that the real authors are not to be spoken about. What Friedman is striving for in *Who Wrote the Bible?* is to uphold the conventional scholarly taboos against imagining the intelligence and creativity of the great Hebraic writers as well as their vibrant culture. But why is the dread of this culture and its writers so strong? It can be only that the culture the writers inhabited was what we today would call a primarily secular culture, only much later appropriated by religion, which succeeded in erasing the original authors' names. Friedman is ultimately not interested in the writers of the Bible at all; rather, he seeks to popularize conventional myths about "religious people" who put the Bible together many years after it was written.

5

A Book Deeply Unread

In *Reading the Book* (1991), Burton Visotzky characterizes his project as "an attempt to open the biblical text to modern interpretation by exposition of an age-old method of reading." That method is midrash, which he defines as a hermeneutic and "communal effort" to search out and find "new meaning" in the Bible. This search for reconnection is a search for a framework of reading or, more precisely, a community of reading. His resource for framing this communal effort is an original community or tradition of reading—rabbinic midrash. Thus, his focus, as he states quite clearly, is "homiletical exegesis" or the " 'reading out' of moral lessons of the age from the Bible."

On the surface there appears to be little to concern us here. Visotzky seems to be on a specialist's terrain, given his specific interest in homiletic reading. But he also claims a broader interest in the creation of interpretive communities, and it is here that we can begin to see what kind of ground we are really on in *Reading the Book*. From the outset, the author makes a promise that a problem of anxiety will be solved. That anxiety is stated in the first sentence of his book: "It just sits there on the shelf." What sits there is the Bible, even though it is, as he puts it, a historical best seller. The anxiety is that something is missing in us that

desires to take it down and read it. And the anxiety extends to a larger
fear that the thing that is missing is also missing in our culture.

What we are told that is missing is a community of reading, and we
are taken back to an older community, that of the rabbis, to learn how
to make such a reading community. Since Visotzky's purpose is to bring
us meaning in the deepest religious and communal sense, it seems hardly
fair to expect him to concern himself with things such as the original
authors of the Bible or the culture that they inhabited. Yet, the promise
of a community of reading is that it will solve a problem in our culture.
Cultural anxiety is a preoccupation of Visotzky's, and interestingly, it
was also one for the rabbinic world. If Visotzky had teased out this anxiety and the resulting strategies of resolution instead of trying to deliver
a model of communal effort, one might have gained a clearer conception of what our real effort must be as a culture and as individual readers. But then he would have had to address what was missing or
repressed in rabbinic reading.

What is ignored by Visotzky, however, is attended to by Moshe Idel
in an essay that first appeared in Hartman and Budick's *Midrash and Literature* (1986). In fact, it is deemed important enough by Idel to form the
context for a discussion of midrashic interpretation and other Jewish literature: "The authoritative rabbinic Jewish texts were regarded as but
pleiades of stars rotating around the Bible, while the other kinds of texts
(apocalyptic, magical, mystical, or mere belles lettres) were successfully
excluded from the rabbinic universe and condemned to total oblivion.
The remnants of the nonrabbinic Jewish literary creations that did survive became planets in Christian literatures; only seldom did they penetrate the rabbinic firmaments. . . . This 'purification' of Jewish literature
contributed to the emergence of the relatively uniform attitude toward
the biblical text." But fragments of these other texts, of other methods
of reading, remained. Moshe Idel has sought to recover them and
reclaim their history and their impact on conventional readings of the
Bible.

Like Gershom Scholem before him, Idel's effort is one of cultural restoration, that is, of trying to recover and confront a lost part of Hebraic culture and Jewish experience—in their case, the kabbalistic counterculture. It is this effort of interpretive restoration that we desperately need to see in action, but unfortunately do not see in Visotzky. Rather than opening the text, we find Visotzky closing it and reopening the firmaments.

Hard as this judgment of Visotzky appears, my natural inclination is to honor the memory of my first reading, in which *Reading the Book* seemed to open up difficult terrain and locate rabbinic culture and midrash in a new way. But to really do this Visotzky would have had to show the individual rabbi at work, grappling with a culture as well as a text. We never see the grappling, the conflict, or the ambiguities of being a rabbinic reader. We see only the rabbis and their romance with the text. And though a few names are attached, this is only to better secure Visotzky's anchor of community and textual romance.

Can we really be satisfied with a sentimental image of the rabbis "as wise and witty readers of the Bible"? Something is lost and avoided in such an image, and to dismiss it as mere sentimentality cuts off analysis prematurely and obscures what is really at stake in *Reading the Book.* It is how we read culture that is at risk and also our understanding of what Lionel Trilling termed the "effort of culture." In Visotzky's book we see the consequences of reading culture through myths of community or, as Trilling explained it, "ideas of man in community." With his images of reading and rabbinic community, Visotzky puts a lid on culture and, most important, the effort behind it—sensibility. And when it threatens to leak out, he plugs it up quickly. Even homiletic-minded rabbis blurred boundaries and played at the edges of texts and culture.

Too much play, however, is dangerous to Visotzky's myths, and he works hard to keep it dammed up, or, as he puts it, "in clear sight": "Since midrashic literature is, above all, interested in lesson teaching, we must keep the rabbinic propensity for blurring story and history in clear sight." The labor here is to keep the lesson and the authority of community unblurred. However, if we lingered awhile in the blurring—the ambiguity and play—we might see a sensibility at work, grappling with the complexities of a culture and a tradition. Why the labor and haste to contain sensibility? Could it be that to linger with the rabbis as sensibilities would bring us too close to other sensibilities, namely, the original authors? It is not unexpected to find Visotzky referring to sources rather than authors of the Bible. It is safe to talk of rabbinic questioning of divine authorship, but to do more would jeopardize his myths of reading and community.

Yet why should we expect him to do more? After all, Visotzky is a rabbi himself, with a declared aim of promoting moral meaning and interpretation. *Reading the Book,* nonetheless, is more than a popularization of a midrashic approach to the Bible. It is a critique of contemporary culture, which at the same time hides the cultural origins of the Bible and suppresses a rabbinic culture that played with those origins even as it sought to protect religious authority.

I seem to be saying that *Reading the Book* perpetrates a deception. Although it is hard to say, it must be said; Visotzky's claims must be engaged because they reach for an authority beyond that of rabbi and religious tradition. This becomes all too apparent as he invites us into his Genesis Seminar reading group, as it will appear on a Bill Moyers TV documentary: a real-life experiment in a community of reading. We are told it is full of "great readers," those who could be called the inventors and interpreters of our contemporary culture—screenwriters, poets, novelists, critics, and translators. Visotzky portrays his Genesis readers as if they are about to become open-air jugglers, risking a vulnerability in order to learn about the Bible—and themselves. But the Genesis Seminar is more about pocket juggling than open-air performance with the biblical text. In fact, the text is the pocket and what is being juggled are its various narratives and narrative techniques. But no authors and no culture.

The seminar is presented as an example of a community of reading in which "we discover that most precious hidden aspect of the biblical text—ourselves." The irony is almost too painful. Instead of our makers of culture discovering their counterparts in an ancient culture, we see them climbing into the pocket of the text. And when something spills out, like an idea of authorship, we see them embarrassed, scrambling to clean up. This is what we witness in Visotzky's vignette in which Max Apple, the fiction writer, blurts out that he would not have written God's command to Abraham as it appears in Genesis 12. According to Visotzky, Apple then "sheepishly" explains his reason why, that "God gives it all away at the outset," that is, promising a reward too soon to Abraham. What is explained away and repocketed deep inside the text is the authorship that Max Apple echoes. For extra measure, Visotzky takes us inside yet another pocket, that of exegesis. Apple can be an "exegete," but not an author when it comes to the Bible.

By the end of *Reading the Book,* everything is in Visotzky's pockets: the Bible, the rabbis, some of our best-known writers and critics, and narrative as well as homily. But then, it is his book and, as an author, he is expected to have pockets. We, however, are led to believe that these are safe, open, and even generous pockets, places where we can come to see ourselves and where all interpretations are welcomed and engaged. Visotzky misrepresents not only the accessibility of his pockets but about what is accessible in the Bible. He claims "uncanny" imagination for the rabbis, the Bible, and the Genesis Seminar, but never for the original authors. Imagination is anchored not in authorship but in the "expansion of narrative" or in "drawing characters who are larger than life."

Still, there seems to be lots of imagination in Visotzky. Genesis Seminar readers are shown applying their writerly imaginations to biblical narrative and building bridges between its stories and techniques and those of film and modern fiction. The rabbis of tradition are shown expanding narrative and "getting behind the biblical text." But when it comes to the original authors of the Bible and their culture, there is no imagination. However, that is just the point; it never comes down to that in *Reading the Book,* even for the writers of the Genesis Seminar. Such things never even come up; J never comes up except as one of several "narrative strands." This is more than a religious taboo in operation. *Reading the Book* is an effort to cover culture with community and control our understanding of the Bible's place in our history and practices.

What is ultimately at stake is a loss unrecovered, a book deeply unread. Without the original authors and their culture, our readings of the Bible are really undoings, discardings of an ancient culture and perhaps our greatest writers. And they are discarding of a chance to know ourselves and revitalize our own culture. This is more, much more than we should be asked to bear in *Reading the Book*, in reading Visotzky.

6

Remasking the Writers of the Bible

There is a moment in *The Postmodern Bible,* a 1995 publication from Yale University Press, in which we are asked, "Just how are we to read the Bible the same way after Auschwitz and Buchenwald?" The question is really an invocation of Emmanuel Levinas and a lead-in to a discussion of how ethics can be restored as a focus for biblical studies and as a frame for reading the Bible. It is interesting that Levinas is more a resource for ethical questioning than for reading in *The Postmodern Bible*—a book all about how we read in the postmodern age. Levinas mostly comes into play in the last chapter on ideological criticism, one of seven "strategies of reading" that include poststructuralism, psychoanalysis, structuralism and narratology, feminist and rhetorical critique, and reader-response criticism. But Levinas is also a reader with a distinctive hermeneutic and, though his *Nine Talmudic Readings* (1990) shows up in the extensive bibliography, it is never addressed in the text.

Of course, ideological criticism brings up things like justice and power in human and political relations. It is understandable that Levinas should make an appearance as ethicist. But as a reader, he has become known for bringing himself and the culture he is in into the act of reading. The phrase "rubbing the text" has come to be associated with him, referring to how his readings are made personal and become a testimony to the effort, the culture behind whatever text is before him. It is an image that he inscribed in "The Temptation of Temptation," one of his Talmudic readings in which he tells of a rabbi who rubbed his foot so hard while studying the Torah that he began to bleed. For Levinas, reading requires that he be present, making himself vulnerable and showing himself at work, "with ears and eyes on the look-out, attentive to the whole . . . open as well to life: the city, the street, other human beings." This is not the kind of reading that frames the concept behind *The Postmodern Bible*. There is no rubbing and certainly no bleeding as the authors come up against the biblical text or even the texts of the postmodern strategists of reading. In fact, the effort is to erase singularity and present a collective authorship, supposedly in keeping with all that is postmodern.

So it is not surprising that when they come to one of the few singular moments in their book, the moment of the question about how to read after the Holocaust, the authors move to a collective, civic concept—that of ethics—instead of moving to the singular and the cultural and the unspeakable loss of both among European Jews during World War II.

The authors behind *The Postmodern Bible* are known as "The Bible and Culture Collective," representing ten male and female academic scholars from the new "interdisciplinary" departments of religion, often called religious or biblical studies. There are no names attached to the chapters, and the intention is to present what is called a "collective argument," defined as a "transforming" critique of biblical scholarship that will bring it into the postmodern struggle with reading and consciousness. Yet it is odd that though there is much talk in the book's introduction about the collective's own struggle with postmodern challenges, we never actually see the struggle, especially the one with consciousness. In defining postmodernism, the collective introduces us to Zygmunt Bauman, who states that it "is no more . . . than the modern mind taking a long, attentive and sober look at itself."

This idea of postmodernism remains an abstract academic concept

throughout a book that claims the following reasons for being written: "We wrote eager to see explicit acknowledgements of ethical
stances, ideological positionings, self-critical and self-reflexive consciousness. . . . Most important, we wrote out of a concern to make
sense of the Bible in a cultural context." I would rather read a first
work by a young scholar like R. Ruth Linden, who shows herself *feeling* her way through the postmodern—because in doing so, she has
grasped what the postmodern calls us to do in our intellectual and cultural efforts: to make ourselves vulnerable, to trace the impress of loss
and origins and go into these makings and tracings. This is what Linden achieves in *Making Stories, Making Selves: Feminist Reflections on the Holocaust* (1993), and it is what "The Bible and the Culture Collective" not
only does not, but fails to even reach for or recognize as its task.

The Postmodern Bible declines to take possession of who they are, and
of who they are reading. Once again we are confronted with an inabil-
ity to take in the complexity of authorship, the complexity of the text.
To see ourselves, sexual human beings, living readers—just as the
authors were, the ones who wrote the Bible.

7

Alter Ego

For Robert Alter, the literary technique of allusion has provided an important window into the Bible as literature. His effort has been to create the context for taking the Bible seriously as "purposeful art" and biblical literary analysis seriously as "rigorous" method. Alter's attention to the Bible's allusive qualities or strategies has been the significant anchor for this effort. And as he takes us into this world of allusion, we are made to feel that we are really getting in touch with the terrain of literary and cultural imagination. There is the sense that as we make contact with allusion, we make contact with the nutrient source of literature and the Bible.

As he talks about allusion in *The World of Biblical Literature* (1993), Alter seems to confirm something fundamental to the literary endeavor: "Allusion, then, is not an embellishment but a fundamental necessity of literary expression: the writer, scarcely able to ignore the texts that have anticipated him and in some sense given him the very idea of writing, appropriates fragments of them, qualifies or transforms them, uses them to give his own work both a genealogy and a resonant background." He follows up, as is his method, with "specific textual cases," or examples. The one that concerns us most immediately is the case of 2 Samuel 13—the rape of Tamar—and its allusions to the story of Joseph in Genesis.

What he hopes to show with his image of the "confluence of allusions" between the two narratives is that there is a purposefulness in the text and, as he elaborates, that "the writer has shaped his meanings by aligning his text with memorable moments in the inherited literary tradition that are at once parallel and antithetical to his own narrative materials." Soon, I should be feeling that sense of contact, of being in touch with the "literary character" of the Bible, as I am brought before the verbal and structural allusions linking the court history and the Joseph story.

When I don't feel it, I wonder why. Maybe it is just the casing of language, that academic style of high objectivity. I could overlook it as a mere distraction if it were just the usual academic frame. But the whole essay feels like a casing, including the very concept of allusion and all its workings. I feel contained instead of in contact. I go back to phrases like "aligning his text," "inherited literary tradition," "at once parallel and antithetical," and I cannot help feeling that something is being devalued. Does a writer ever align his text, make "use of" things like allusion and tradition? Reading such phrases makes one want to flee to the observations of someone who is a poet as well as a critic, the late Edwin Denby, for instance. And I literally do, in trying to find out why I am not feeling what I am supposed to be feeling as I read Alter. I find it in two essays: "Balanchine Choreographing" and "Dancers, Buildings and People in the Street." In the first, Denby gives us details but he also gives us the rare context of a sensibility at work, so that the details congeal into a work of art—in this case a ballet in the making—and put us into contact with the work of creating and the hand and mind behind it, namely Balanchine. The second is about how to do criticism, about seeing—what goes into seeing or experiencing a work of art. In these essays, one comes into contact with how dance is created through the effort of a critic who, as Frank O'Hara expressed it, "is always there, telling you what he sees and hears and feels," giving us "an equation in which attention equals Life." With Alter, however, we get an equation in which attention equals death—the death of art and sensibility. His details are devoid of any sense of how writers actually create a literary work. Most important, they are emptied out of the sensibility behind the work.

Again and again we see Alter dismissing, with a deliberate offhandedness, the original authors. Yet whether it is the editors or the authors, it matters little, for as Alter states, "In my view scholarship has seriously overstated the difference." And where the device of allusion is concerned, what jumps out at any sensitive reader is the absence of the fundamental sense of play that motivates any great writing. Play with what? In great literature, it is the nature of intimacy that is probed and revealed, and almost always this work is reflected in a friendly—even intimate—competition among writers of the same rank. It is highly likely that J and S were two such writers, intimate with each other's works.

In the writings of J and S, consider the question of who came first, Joseph or Tamar. Can we get by with superficial readings by critics that assume the Joseph story was part of a tradition that S made "use of"? It is just as likely that J read S's story of Tamar and played off it in her version of the Joseph story. The crucial point here is not to define which came first—an impossible academic exercise—but to become sensitive to the intimate play between two great authors.

But why not just leave it as "two great texts"—why do I insist on authorship? Without the sense of an artistic genius at work, literary analysis becomes an assimilative force, absorbing singularity and culture into an "overarching unity," an "ideological continuity." These are concepts created by Alter to blind us to the existence of S, or any author who did not follow a "consensus" (what great author would?). Authorship boils down in Alter to an insignificant diversity: "But for all this diversity, there is also a kind of elastic consensus that expresses itself in certain shared values and concepts, accompanied by a shared set of images, idioms, model figures, and exemplary stories. For all we know, there may have been a Hebrew literature that operated outside this consensus and that did not survive. Within the consensus, allusion was a natural means of reinforcing ideological continuity across schools and eras."

Alter goes on to distinguish his view of the use of allusion in the Bible from those who represent it as formulaic or mechanical. The effect is to make us feel that something has been gained, that the biblical text has increased in value with Alter's attention to allusion. By this point, however, we see what Alter is after in opposing "mechanical" and "purposeful." The hero of this story of allusion is the redactor, the individual or community of individuals who pulled the "sundry texts" together into a "purposeful," consensual whole. To celebrate allusion is to celebrate the redactor. And more important, it is to celebrate Professor Robert Alter—our new redactor of the biblical text.

If that sounds like an indictment, I am afraid that it is. It is not merely that Alter cannot see J or S or is disabled in some way from reading a literary work and its culture. I am afraid that Alter is much more purposeful than that. And I say "afraid" because I am—I cannot quite believe what I witness in this essay. When I read "For all we know, there may have been a Hebrew literature that operated outside . . . that did not survive," I feel like something has been lost, suppressed all over again. This is not the usual academic dullness, but an active effort to dull the thinking and imagination of the reader to that "Hebrew literature that operated outside," the remnants of which do in fact survive in what we have, for example, of J and S. More important, what Alter dulls us to is the thought that what was outside was inside: that there existed a literary culture in ancient Israel that was not at the margins but at the center of a civilization. And that what was outside, and made its way inside only much later, was the religious culture of the redactor.

With allusion, Alter puts a lid on the culture of J and S and any feeling for the vulnerability and openness to challenge that characterize the play of great writers in a creative culture. The closest he gets to the subject of culture is when he invokes the image of a scribal culture. He puts it in quotations—"scribal culture"—to distance himself from the apparent put-down, which is the idea that such a culture would not be up to the kind of "dynamic" use of allusion that he is portraying. After all, allusion illustrates "the complex means used by the biblical writers to lock their texts together." T. S. Eliot is summoned forth as a modern-day example of the kind of dynamic and complex usage that Alter has in mind. But would we think of Eliot as locking his texts together with Shakespeare or Milton? Can we take seriously a reader like Alter, who takes the allusions of Eliot so seriously? As Donald Hall has noted in his book *Remembering Poets* (1977), Eliot had a sense of comedy about his role as a man of letters, and his perpetrations of it were "lost on almost everyone."

They weren't lost on Dorothy Parker, though she was bored by them. We are reminded of this by Ann Douglas in *Terrible Honesty* (1995) and of how Eliot was "a supreme trickster," sending many a critic to the library to look up his allusions and citations, like those in "The Waste Land," which he called "a remarkable composition of bogus scholarship." This is not the kind of dynamic that Alter has in mind when it comes to Eliot's work or the Bible. Alter's kind of dynamic turns literature into "a resource to be drawn on again and again for the shifting expressive needs of a purposeful art." There is a deadness in this image of literature. Is this really how a literary culture thrives, or is it a picture of another kind of culture, one that draws together and puts together "sundry texts"? Is this art or artfulness? The distinction would be lost on someone who talks in terms of "T.S. Eliot alludes to"—or for whom allusion is "dictated by the self-recapitulative logic of literary expression." Of more significance, however, is what is lost to us in Alter's world of allusion as it pertains to the Bible.

In trying to understand what is lost, I found myself consulting Allen Mandelbaum's afterword to his translation of Ovid's *Metamorphoses* (1993). It is interesting to note that he begins by referring to the last word of the work—*vivam*—meaning "I shall live" or "I shall have life." It is more than a matter of how he begins, it is that Mandelbaum *knows* where to begin. Ovid is speaking of the poet's life, his impact: "if poets' prophecies are ever right—/my name and fame are sure." We can think of a poet's prophecy as imaginative power; it is a literary work's life force. And so Mandelbaum knows right away what he must confront in a work such as the *Metamorphoses:* its author and his life force—his imaginative work. He also knows he cannot do justice to this life force without imagining it in a context of play with the author's contemporaries or peers.

Thus we see Ovid in Rome and in the circle of other poets, such as Horace. Mandelbaum is helped in this effort by Ovid himself, who left behind an autobiographical poem detailing certain facets of his life. Unfortunately, we have nothing so obvious from J or S. But does that leave us empty-handed? Readers of the Bible like Alter seem to think so. In the first chapter to *The World of Biblical Literature,* Alter states that "biblical tradition itself went to great lengths to hide the tracks of the individual author." This is the beginning of his explanation of what sets the Bible apart from any other literary work in Western civilization. His aim is to build a metaphor: the Bible as "A Peculiar Literature." The motive behind this metaphor becomes clear when we read his account of the "anonymity of the biblical writer and the absence of context for him": "There is no proclamation of authorship . . . no hint of any individual writer aspiring to eternal fame through literary achievement. Instead, the writer disappears into the tradition, makes its voice his, or vice versa." Alter stages these passages as if he is merely reporting on the facts, when in actuality he is advancing a highly speculative theory of his own about how authors of the Bible disappeared. Hidden in this reportage is a claim—that the writers of the Bible did not want their names known.

However, it is far more likely that the great ones such as J and S, highly individualized in their art, wrote for an audience of peers—just as the great writers of Elizabethan England and Ovid's Rome wrote for their fellow courtiers and paid little attention to book publication. When we read of Ovid's exile and banishment, we feel even luckier to have the *Metamorphoses* and can only wonder at what might have been lost. It is this kind of wondering that Alter hopes to seal off in his reportage of "hide the tracks of" and disappearing writers. Is it not the critic's role to attempt to uncover these tracks rather than throwing something else on top of them? What Alter throws on top is another myth—an academic one—that parallels the religious myth that developed about six centuries after the original writers were dead.

The religious tradition that erased their names is completely different from the culture that produced the divine writings of J and S. One can conclude only that Alter's agenda is to erase any speculation that is not his own, any movement of thought that might unseal the imaginative resources or "vivam" of writers who are not in his own image of academic commentator. His myth is that these writers wished to disappear into a nameless whole called "the biblical world," where everything is foreign, including "our practice of reading for pleasure." But what we see in his book is that as the literature of the Bible becomes more and more "peculiar," Alter himself becomes more and more indispensable.

Central to the "stubborn peculiarity" of the biblical text is what is described as its "composite nature." This concept of Alter's is nothing new, but here we see him dressing it up as "collage." We might wonder whom this dress is for. It seems to be for us, a way to give us access to the peculiar fancies of the Bible. Yet, in fact it is a dress for the original writers, who are first corseted into a national tradition of "circulating" texts and then made to give the audience of the time what we are told was not only expected but "accepted"—a composite performance. Once again we see the original writers disappearing into a tradition. And even though Alter makes an effort to distance himself from other dressmakers called into question by *The Book of J,* such as those who celebrate the integrating designs of the redactor, he still ends up preferring their "excesses" to those who would let the original authors be the designers and dressmakers.

Ovid's *Metamorphoses* could be described by Alter as a collage of classical myths. But would we be satisfied with a critic who remembered it as an artful composite, with credits to Rome and its circulating texts, the

patron Messalla Corvinus, and the "synthesizing imagination" of scholars and scribes? The *Metamorphoses* is the work that it is because of a powerful sensibility who authored it and who was irreverent in his play with
myth and convention. In fact it is the element of play in Ovid's sensibility that Mandelbaum leaves us with in his discussion of the work. It
is one thing to call forth a textual collage and quite another to call forth
an artist at play with his materials. As Mandelbaum puts it, "all that is
here is not all that seems. Ovid's fictions form a bacchanalian narrative
revel, in which each element may be drunk or delirious, but which—in
its endless deceptions—provides truth." The truth of Ovid; the truth of
J and S. It is this truth, this personal commitment of a powerful author
that Alter would cover up and hide from us in a composite text.

My purpose here is to make the reader ask *why*. Most of us do not
know our own resources, nor do we know our own economies. And this
not knowing is what scholars like Alter count on, and what great
thinkers and scientists, like Freud, try to remedy. We could describe
Freud's lifework as a steady attempt to equip us so that "we can bear it
if a few of our expectations turn out to be illusions." This is a quote from
The Future of an Illusion, which is primarily about our wishes as a culture
and as individuals. His aim is not to do away with that wishing part of
us, but to develop the resources to look at it, to look at all the versions
of ourselves, to understand "how the world must appear to us in consequence of the particular character of our organization." In perhaps his
seminal work, *The Interpretation of Dreams*, Freud developed a process to
bring us closer to the "character of our organization" and closer to our
own resources as individuals and as a species. He was unafraid to let us
see his mind at work in developing this process and unafraid as well to
let us see him draw on imagination and the imaginative resources of
literary authors. Freud understood that any project of knowing requires
some effort to imagine what is not known.

Here is the risk of being at the frontier of any experimental or interpretive science. As readers of the Bible poised on the twenty-first cen-

tury, we need to approach this frontier, but scholars like Alter do not have the resources to guide us, nor do they wish to take us there. If anything, their wish is to disable our own resources by numbing us to the resources of those already at the frontier—the original writers. Allusion is one of the anesthetizing agents. What we become insensible to in Alter's world of allusion is the presence and complexity of an author. When invited into this world, the reader must ask *why*. Why talk in such terms? What is behind it? Would we talk about Euripides in terms of allusion? Or would we speak of him as William Arrowsmith speaks of him in his foreword to W. S. Merwin and George Dimock's translation of *Iphigenia at Aulis* (1978)—as one fully possessed of his materials as an artist and vitally engaged with a culture? Why is Arrowsmith able to talk about the interplay of Euripides and Homer without encasing it in allusion?

We read authors like Robert Lowell for their translations because we sense they know what is at stake. In a prefatory note to his translation of the *Oresteia* by Aeschylus (1978), Lowell wrote: "No version of the Oresteia, even a very great one, such as Marlowe or Milton might have written, can be anything like what was performed first in Athens with music, dance, masks, and an audience of thirty thousand or more—an event we cannot recover and something no doubt grander than any play we can see." What is important to note here is that Lowell's reference point is the play's presence in a culture. His effort of translation was about making the loss of that presence felt. And the other side of that loss, that presence, was a sensibility. Lowell made himself vulnerable to making the loss of that sensibility felt in his translations. Sensibility and culture, their loss and imaginative restoration, was what Lowell knew to be at stake at the frontier of literature.

These are also our stakes at the frontier of the Bible. But what is at the frontier is obscured when we have a critic who distorts even the small distance we have traveled in biblical studies. It is one thing to criticize imaginative restorations like *The Book of J* that merely use source criticism as a starting point. But it is quite another to characterize nineteenth- and twentieth-century efforts to illuminate sources as following a "risky road of conjecture." Alter thinks he can actually erase authorship from the landscape by tying it to epistemological questions in the work of those who pursued source criticism. He cites Gabriel Josipovici's critique of what is described as the "nineteenth-century bias toward seeking the truth in origins." And for extra measure, he imports Derrida—a thinker he has no liking for and certainly no understanding of—to support his own "conjecture" that there is nothing that can be really known about origins, especially the origins of ancient texts.

Alter's purpose is to support a claim that is presented as a matter of fact, that "what we most dependably possess is the text framed by tradition." The reader must ask why there is this reaction to a search for origins, not to mention a serious imaginative search such as that found in *The Book of J.* I do not think it risks too much conjecture to explore this resistance as a reactionary response to what Freud described as the "biological blow" delivered by Darwin in the nineteenth century, followed by the "psychological blow" begun by psychoanalysis into the twentieth century, in *The Resistances to Psychoanalysis* (1925). These were turning points in our understanding of the importance of origins, and we are in the midst of the next—the ecological blow of the late twentieth and twenty-first centuries. Alter's resistance to origins is so strong that he co-opts Derrida to make it seem like an impossible project. But this is a mischaracterization of Derrida, who has tried to make our struggle with origins more complex but not pointless. Derrida's effort has been to make individual minds resistant to complexity disappear—not to erase individual minds. He has relentlessly pursued the complexity of origins by struggling with authors who possess a powerful, singular sensibility. Derrida is not afraid of such an individual. But is Robert Alter? Can he remain in the midst of someone more imaginative than he is?

Of course, it is a deception to criticize the idea of authorship by attacking the scholars of source criticism. They were interested in identifying the sources of the Bible—the different documentary strands—

not the original authors. But what we must ask ourselves is why Alter avoids an argument with *The Book of J* on its own terms. Why does he discuss the book with a positivistic or methodological lens instead of engaging it as a work of imaginative restoration? To do so, he would have to take us out into the field, where the work of restoration comes alive. The reader never learns about the nature of this work or the nature of translations at the frontier of this work, such as *The Book of J.* Instead, there are only detours where what the reader learns about such books is that they remain fixated on "individual literary imagination," which by this point Alter hopes has become a sufficiently taboo subject for the reader. And enough so that the reader will accept his next claim as fact—that "it is questionable whether any one of the strands of the biblical text is really a unitary literary artifact, reflecting a single author and a single moment in time." To ensure the taboo, he tries to remove the Bible from our literary experience. This is the motive behind his metaphor of the Bible as a peculiar literature. But the reader must ask why Alter is so intent on disallowing our experience of Western narratives.

The answer becomes clear as he invokes the story of King David as illustration. Having provided a general picture of how he thinks the Bible came to be a composite text, Alter then claims that the story of David is "built on a textual matrix utterly unlike that of any of the later major narratives of the West." The reader is left believing that the books of Samuel are all of one piece, and is never told that there is one narrative highly distinguishable from the rest—that said to be written by the Court Historian, or S. We can conclude only that Alter disallows Western literary experience in order to absorb the court history of David and its author into a compositeness and peculiarity that only he has access to. For to admit our literary resources as readers would permit a freedom of inquiry in which his claims and taboos could not survive.

It is ironic that even as Alter forecloses modern literary experience to us he draws on it for himself. We have already seen how he invokes T. S. Eliot's use of allusion to give credence to his story of how it is used in the Bible. And we have seen how limited his understanding of Eliot's allusive play really is. But it is important to realize that we are being blinded to something fundamentally important in understanding the relationship between authors such as J and S. When Alter speaks of Eliot's use of allusion, it is in terms of a citation of another literary period, that represented by Shakespeare. Actually, all his references are of allusions between generations. But to fix Eliot in this way is to conceal from us the fact that Eliot's allusions to his contemporaries are far more significant than those to writers of another century. And what we lose is yet another chance to see how authors seriously play. They play in a culture with their creative peers.

The poet Frank O'Hara reminds us of this in works of criticism which capture his interplay with the abstract expressionists and also other authors, particularly John Ashbery. And W. H. Auden reminds us of it in his essay on the poet C. P. Cavafy. His primary focus is on the intellectual intimacy between two living writers. Auden, beginning with himself and Cavafy, shows how it is enacted in Cavafy's work. He directs us to "The First Step," where Cavafy makes a literary culture of contemporaries come alive. It is interesting that Auden never refers to allusion in his essay in order to make the presence of a literary culture felt. His biggest problem is to convey to the reader how he can access a poetic work that he can read only in translation. He tells us that it is because something carries through, something remains alive: "Something I can only call, most inadequately, a tone of voice, a personal speech. I have read translations of Cavafy made by many different hands, but every one of them was immediately recognizable as a poem by Cavafy; nobody else could possibly have written it."

We could say the same for the work of J and S. But Auden's ear is not Alter's. Auden is attuned not to editors or redactors but to an imaginative, singular sensibility and his creative culture. Alter's ear is deaf not only to the original writers but also to the culture that they inhabited, a fatal flaw in a critic. While he apparently reads the Hebrew of the biblical tradition very well, he seems insecure with early Hebrew, as if he has not mastered the history of the language and its origins, so different from later or postexilic Hebrew. Without a knowledge of origins, and without an understanding of cuneiform and the great era of translation into the original Hebrew alphabet, Alter is at pains to hide his scholarly defects by rejecting the responsibility to imagine a culture of great Hebrew writers.

8

Primitive Studies

At the end of McCarter's consideration of the narrative sources in 2 Samuel, he notes his obligation to direct the reader to "the growing number of scholars who are investigating the narratives of II Samuel from a more strictly literary point of view." He makes no sustained attempt to engage this literary approach, just to acknowledge the scholarship and make recommendations from the literature. One of those recommendations is D. M. Gunn's study of the succession narrative which the reader is told argues for "a fuller appreciation of its nature as a story." At this point, the reader is forced to realize that nothing more is to be gleaned from McCarter and the Anchor Bible about the succession narrative as an authored work of literature.

The study recommended is *The Story of King David: Genre and Interpretation* (1982). The reader is immediately heartened as Gunn promises an alternative view of the succession narrative that emphasizes its primary character as a "work of art and entertainment." Gunn seems to share an impatience with efforts to categorize the succession narrative as didactic or wisdom literature, political propaganda, or history writing. Unlike other scholars, he is able to take a stand for the succession narrative as a work of art and seems angered by attempts to subordinate that understanding "to other postulated dimensions of the document." How disturbing, then, to reach the next sentence in Gunn's introduction: "While a term such as 'novel' is not entirely inappropriate as a classification, an exploration of stereotyped patterns and motifs in the story suggests that the story has a more traditional character . . . a tradition of Israelite story-telling which was most probably originally an oral one." Disturbance turns to dismay as it becomes all too clear why Professor Gunn prefers not to characterize the narrative as a novel: "The term implies an essentially written as opposed to an oral genre, and it implies also a particularly high degree of autonomy of the author over his style and subject matter."

To characterize the narrative as a novel, then, would require that Professor Gunn confront an author and that is precisely what he cannot do and what he will apparently avoid, like the scholars he critiques, at all cost. Even more disappointing is how Gunn seems to have no idea about how to characterize great writing and literature. He is so uncomfortable with the idea of genre that he actually takes refuge in "story" as genre. Somehow the classification of "story" offers cover, protection from that "autonomy" of authorship that Gunn, like other scholars, seems to fear. He expects us to believe that S was incapable of playing with or redefining any one of many genres.

As is commonplace with all great writers, the conventional notion of genre is broken or expanded. And certainly the S writer is no less sophisticated than a Sophocles or Shakespeare. But where great writers bend genre, academic scholars always try to straighten everything to fit a genre. As Gunn instructs the reader, genre is a guide to conventions and expectations, or what Gunn calls "traditional motifs." Yet it is not and cannot be a guide to an author, especially one like S, who breaks expectations. So Gunn's book is bulging with definitions of the elements of genre, but his interpretation of the succession narrative as a "work of art and entertainment" is missing an author. However, this is not surprising once we realize that Gunn, like his fellow scholars, is filling up a space of anxiety with academic definitions, and that his characterization of genre fills up what has been emptied out by our cultural and academic taboos.

Excavations of oral traditions and traditional motifs do seem to promise enrichment and a recovery of ancient sources. But they, too, are strategies of depletion. Invocations of oral traditions empty out the written text, disposing of any irony or complexity that might suggest an intelligent author or an author's unique intelligence. The myth of an oral tradition is always a convenient defense for scholars unable to imagine a great author. And the folly of such narrow thinking about authorship becomes apparent when we compare written biblical text to oral (texts) traditions in neighboring cultures. It is a commonplace for scholars to categorize oral texts as primitive. However, as recent scholarship in other fields now reveals, primitive cultures often produce the greatest complexity in their arts.

It is now apparent that to resort to such scholarly myths as oral or primitive traditions is a repression—more strongly, a whitewash—of cultures that produce great authors such as S. That is why, to our grave disappointment, Gunn goes on to repress the notion of a momentous Hebraic culture that could produce powerful and idiosyncratic artists and authors.

Yet Gunn might say he is making room for something that has been squeezed out by other scholars. What he thinks he is making room for is an oral tradition and a story of "serious entertainment." He takes considerable labor to explain that his classification of the succession narrative as an oral-traditional text does not foreclose the existence of what he calls "a creative narrator": "The description of a narrative as 'traditional' does not imply that the author has *no* personal control over his material or is totally unable or unwilling to innovate; rather, it indicates that the composer works with influences or constraints regarding style and content that are relatively greater than is generally the case with modern novel writing." But just who is this "creative narrator" of an "oral-traditional text"? According to Gunn's "concluding observations," this "creative narrator" of "serious entertainment" did not realize that his work was "one of fiction . . . the author believed himself to be recounting in essence what actually happened." At this point, the reader can only shake his head at the folly of consulting Gunn, and of taking McCarter's literature review to heart. Far from being helpful and liberating, Gunn's book turns out to fit the suffocating genre of academese. The question for us, though, is can we rest content with biblical studies while we go without critics of ancient cultures like the engaging Italian, Roberto Calasso, who understand that great authors interrogate the conventions and complexities in which they live?

Gunn might reply that he is arguing for a "creative narrator." And yet he leaves us with a cardboard character. How can we take seriously an author who is unaware of his fictions—disconnected from himself as an artist? But perhaps the better question is how can we take Gunn seriously as a reader of literature or as a student of so-called primitive cultures. I do not believe we can or that we can afford to, especially when it comes to our aboriginal and prehistoric origins. The latest discoveries of Ice Age art in the caves of Cosquer and Chauvet in southeastern France confound the way we think of Paleolithic people. As announcements reached the popular press in the summer of 1995, the tone was one of fascination but underneath was a disturbing anxiety. The task of reimagination has been difficult.

Even those who have a lifetime of intellectual intimacy with other caves of Paleolithic art have been hard pressed to know how to begin. One who has tried is Alexander Marshack, an elder archaeologist who has asked that we consider the intelligence and culture behind the art. Yet how disappointing when we read that all that is interesting to him is the development of meaning, that is, how human intelligence and culture came to produce images that carried meaning and reflected thought. In his description of these paintings there is no sense or imagining of the hand or sensibility behind them. His discussion of the new discoveries in the July/August 1995 issue of *Archaeology* is billed as "Ice

Age Imagery: What Did It Mean?" Inside his article, we find the art reduced to image, sensibility reduced to ritual and tradition. And we find the inevitably tiresome question of how the caves "were used and why they were decorated"—a parallel to the obsession of biblical scholars with the religious usage of the text.

One is reminded again of how far we have to go in our conceptions of the primitive. Mary Douglas gave it a strong try in an article in the winter 1982 issue of *Daedalus*, when she chided religious-studies scholars for their assumptions about the primitive: "Everything is wrong because the stereotype of premoderns is wrong. It has been constructed to flatter prejudged ideas. Some premoderns are indeed organized according to the stereotype . . . but some of them are as mobile, footloose, and uncommitted as any modern academic." Of course, what is fun and ironic in Douglas's essay is how modern academics show themselves to be less modern, less in touch with their own culture, less able to see themselves than the premoderns that are their subjects. Yet, more ironically, Douglas calls on these scholars to modernize, to develop a self-consciousness equal to those they study. If only Marshack could see himself in the art of his subjects, or, rather, risk to imagine the knowledge lost to him as a modern man. Instead, he gives us a sad display of a paleo-sensibility stripped of the talent for intimate and startling translations of the life processes of other species. This is also, finally, what is insufferable in Gunn's study—to be left as we are, without an author who knows his work, and who can see himself and his culture in that work.

9

Erasures of Hebraic Spirit

While Gunn wishes to protect the story in the succession narrative, Joel Rosenberg wants to preserve its argument, that is, its allegorical and explanatory value. Where Gunn clings to a "creative narrator," albeit "traditional," Professor Rosenberg pursues a text that is so much in possession of its social, political, and religious signification that "we have little choice but to regard the text itself, for all practical purposes, as the 'author,' quite without need of a term like 'redactor.' " Accordingly, Gunn's anchor of "art and entertainment" and oral tradition is not enough. The story becomes a diversion instead of something that a people value for its power to explain, talk back to them, and reinterpret their cultural understandings. In this view, a story must be meaningfully situated to embody its full value, and it is this full-bodiedness that Professor Rosenberg argues for in *King and Kin: Political Allegory in the Hebrew Bible* (1986).

One way to consider this book is in the context of an effort in the interpretive sciences to revise our understanding of rationality, art, and human agency by reconstructing how they are fundamentally situated or, in the words of Thomas McCarthy, "embodied, culturally mediated, and interwoven with social practice." To think of the book in this way would call to mind philosophers like Hans-Georg Gadamer and his idea that we are always emerging from a state of being "thrown" into a tradition. We must proceed in our interpretations with a sense of a historical or rooted consciousness, a context of meaning. This has spawned a worthwhile body of literature, especially for those in academia trying to move beyond confinements or dichotomies of thought like relativism and objectivism. In a way, thinkers like Gadamer have sought a full-bodiedness for the human sciences. And while we can appreciate Professor Rosenberg's effort to claim the same for the narratives of the Bible and for biblical scholarship in general, we must still wonder at how he seeks a full-bodiedness for everything in his book except the original authors.

This full-bodiedness is what is described as "the system of thought 'in' which the texts are embedded." He calls this the "intelligence" of textual composition, which he says is closer at hand than the original authors of the Yahwist narrative and court history, J and S: "All we have is the text, and so the questions we must pose are questions about the properties of the text." He defines his task of interpretation as allegorical and concerned with revealing this "system of thought." We may well ask how a disembodied intelligence can be so full-bodied in Professor Rosenberg's estimation. There is a certain pathos at work as we see him attuning himself to what he calls "the anonymous traditionary voice that underlies all voices, human and divine, under whose rubric books begin and end, things are brought to pass, persons are made to speak." It is tempting to think of Heidegger here, but instead I will keep to Gadamer, who calls us to the pathos of "the hermeneutical circle," in which we allow ourselves to be spoken to by texts and traditions, works of art and literature. The aim is to establish a movement in this circle between traditions or modes of consciousness that we belong to and those that we do not.

But there is a danger in a science of ontology that does not take account of a natural and physical history and, I might add, a case history. Self-knowledge is a part of the hermeneutic movement, but can we come to see ourselves out of the space and time of our inner worlds and our evolutionary histories? The pathos of Professor Rosenberg promises to fill us up, but our subsistence is to be gotten in the circle of "an anonymous traditionary voice," where we are told that "we approach the 'who' of biblical composition": a "presence" called "we," a "corporate selfhood," an "'Israel' self-aware . . . sadly wise." Can we be filled by such readings of "Israel," disembodied of the play of authors and artists who created the metaphor and the culture?

In *The Book of J*, Professor Joel Rosenberg was noted by Harold Bloom as going "further than Speiser in reading Genesis and 2 Samuel as companion works." I am afraid that I must differ on this point and argue that Professor Rosenberg, if anything, sets us back in this task. Speiser was much further ahead because he could conceive that the problem of J and S was one of imagination and that it would take another imaginative author—like J herself—to do the work of restoring these original authors. For Joel Rosenberg, the texts of J and S are companions in the sense of being part of the corporate traditionary body, where "all is placed with care before our eyes, then gathered to its place of rest within the larger fabric of tradition." The keeper of this body is what he calls the "traditionary collector" who safeguards "each inherited element" in the stories while "seeking an arrangement of elements that would make a statement of its own." In the anonymous traditionary body, there is no need for J or S, because what keeps this body animated is the "artistry of editing," the "system of thought" in "redactional art."

Professor Rosenberg not only dissolves J and S into the traditionary body but also tries to take Shakespeare in as well. His way in is through allegory which points to a mediating, traditionary intelligence that holds together a "system of relations," the primary relation being between the biblical text and a "readership concerned with Israel's politics and history." A similar relation is envisioned between the Shakespearean text and its "Tudor or Stuart audience." D. M. Gunn acknowledged this relation for both the court history and the "historical" plays of Shakespeare. But for him, the political and historical elements in Shakespearean plays were its "subject-matter" and would not distract him from the fact that "they are above all *plays*, works of art." The distinction is lost on Professor Rosenberg, who criticizes Gunn for clinging "to a belief in the autonomy of art." What matters instead is the "integrated argument," the "political import," that is, the relations that bind a public consciousness. Without these relations, without the allegorical translation, Professor Rosenberg cannot reach the fullness of meaning that he seeks. And he cannot reach the traditional body where he evidently longs to be. But should we join him there?

Several centuries after the great biblical writers did their work, the group power of religious institutions in ancient Israel—often mixed up with political authority—began a process of devaluing the identity of these writers. Even today we can witness the same impulse in books like *King and Kin*. Professor Rosenberg sets out innocently to enlighten us about the political consciousness of the biblical text. But we end up in a traditional body, where we are made to believe that everyone wants to be, including the original biblical authors who had to commit some sort of literary suicide for the larger philosophical and political agenda in order to be there. The Bible may represent many different things to different people, but literature is not about a subject. A subject is what literature uses to create art. If a subject uses art instead of vice versa, then a work may be political, sociological, or of one of the other didactic disciplines, but certainly not art. There is much more chance that a work created by a chimpanzee will be art, since that chimpanzee at least understands, far more than some of our current biblical scholars, that his primary task is to play with his medium.

The knowledge of how to play with one's medium is what many would say distinguishes an artist. Recently, during a visit to the Metropolitan Museum of Art to see the work of Jackson Pollock, the sculptor Richard Serra made a comparison to a show of children's art that he had seen. In an interview by Michael Kimmelman appearing in *The New York Times* on August 11, 1995, Serra observed, "What I saw there and what you see here is what you seldom see in American painting: an exuberance in the act of making, in the sheer pleasure of playing with materials." In that observation, Serra defined the experience that I had of being in the midst of his own sculpture called "Serpentine," of being in the midst of a powerful and complex sensibility. This is an experience, however, that will not be found in the traditionary body of Professor Rosenberg. It is an experience to be had only in the midst of J and S and with those readers with the imagination to stay in their midst.

It is helpful to consider Joel Rosenberg's critique of Gunn in light of the work by a contemporary author like Tony Kushner and his recent play *Angels in America*. It is subtitled "A Gay Fantasia on National Themes," and it is easy to imagine that S's work could have been thought of as a gay fantasia at certain moments as well, though "gay" most likely would not have carried the same meanings. (Or perhaps it would have.) During its production on Broadway, many of the critics focused on the "national themes," almost forgetting the rest of the subtitle. Many chose to think of the play as political commentary, as a demonstration of political consciousness about the terms of community. But this fantasia is about the workings of a sensibility and his or her interplay with a culture. What was important about *Angels in America* was less the interplay of political themes and more the writer's play with the history of theater and playwrights, that is, with other sensibilities.

Yes, the play can be seen as a blurring of the boundaries between life and death as posed by AIDS and a subculture's experience of it. And it can be seen as a satire of the common conventions of what and where that boundary is. But it is most startling as a play on the history of the theater's engagement with those boundaries and, most of all, as a work by a writer who knows his materials well enough to play with them. It is the full-bodiedness of his sensibility—a fully sexualized author—that we absorb at play with other sensibilities of his time. This is a kind of full-bodiedness that we can imagine as well in J and S. But it is the kind that biblical scholars like Joel Rosenberg hope to erase in order to protect themselves from the true Hebraic spirit.

What is this spirit? It is not the absorbing univocal voice of normative tradition or "redactional art," but the polyvocal, human voices of authors who put themselves personally at stake in the expansion of genres and the working of their fantasias on normative tradition.

10

Confronting an Author

Ryken and Longman's *A Complete Literary Guide to the Bible* (1993), was written in reaction to Alter and Kermode's *The Literary Guide to the Bible*. The provocation, according to Ryken and Longman, was that Alter and Kermode seemed to promise with their title "a definitive and thorough-going literary approach to the Bible," but in the end failed to deliver a "systematic literary method." Ryken and Longman's aim was to correct this deficiency and provide a "consistency in method" and an integration of literary and biblical analysis. They make it clear that they asked contributors to avoid certain subjects such as "historicity of events" and "theories of authorship."

At first it is understandable that the editors should exercise care that their anthology not sink into academic, or, as they put it, "faddish" the-orizing about such trivial things as authors. They explain that their effort is to ensure that theory not become a diversion from the text or a stage for scholarly exhibitionism. Thus, it is supposed to be reassuring to hear their concern for linking theory with practice. Preoccupations with theory and practice are symptomatic of the postmodern challenge. Unfortunately, Ryken and Longman's engagement with the theory-practice link is best described as a platform for presenting a caricature—born of profound resentment—of literary analysis in general and postmodern instigations in particular. But more important for our concerns, it is yet another strategy for dodging the culture and authors that produced such great writing as S's succession narrative.

From their introduction, the reader learns that "literature enacts rather than states, shows rather than tells." They invoke Flannery O'Connor to explain that "the storyteller speaks *with* character and action, not *about* character and action." Their effort here is to demonstrate that literature requires interpretation, that the human experience is interpreted through story and metaphor. We absorb with anticipation their point that literature is marked by "self-conscious artistry" and that underlying the range of critical literary approaches is "a shared conviction that literature is the result of conscious composition." The aim is to move ever closer to the text, to create an intimacy with the text. However, since they are unable to discuss the consciousness behind a "conscious composition," Ryken and Longman must anchor this wish, this ocean of feeling, in something, and, as expected, it is in what they term "the historical function of the biblical text."

For Ryken and Longman, history is something real and something safe. In many ways their book is a kind of safe place for what they call "traditional historical-critical methods," a place safeguarded for history and the historical approach and a respect for traditional scholarship. But at this point, if not sooner, the reader has realized that this commentary on literature is a sentimental refrain, a backdrop for academic skirmishing and for yet another attempt at disciplinary reform. As with most sentimentality, something is being repressed ever deeper while something else is being worshiped and enshrined. What Ryken and Longman hope to show is that they have and possess the text, and that the reader must go through them to reach it. They intend to supplant Alter as king of the text-retentive hill.

How should we respond to this need to grasp and hold the text so tightly? Most of all, how can we explain this notion that it can be held and grasped without delivering an author?

The tone of this book is designed to be reassuring, aimed at restoring an equilibrium where we can once again find sustenance in matters such as "plot, character, setting, point of view, and diction." But this is an equilibrium that the editors can sustain only by suppressing the original authors and any challenge to normative tradition. What does it mean when *A Complete Literary Guide to the Bible* cannot even refer to *The Book of J* by name but instead puts its coauthor, Harold Bloom, on a list of unpious readers now in fashion? It is not unexpected that Ryken and Longman should name the titles of books they like and suppress the naming of those they do not. But this very characteristic raises the question of why they name the titles associated with Robert Alter when they claim he causes them so much vexation. The answer is found at the end of the same section where *The Book of J* goes nameless. Ryken quotes at length from Alter's book on literary theory, *The Pleasures of Reading in an Ideological Age*. And from the quote it is clear that more is shared with Robert Alter than we were led to believe. Ryken refers to this book because it seeks what he and Longman seek: an interpretive equilibrium supported by what Alter describes as "the world of experience outside the text" and the "formal resources of literary expression." But whose world is this and whose formality? It is not accidental that we should be directed to reading pleasures available in "an Ideological Age." These are pleasures that can be provided by a redactor, both ancient and contemporary. For Alter, Ryken, and Longman, these are stable pleasures because the text is secured by normative anchors.

But the pleasures in this equilibrium float on top a great fear that we should discover another kind of age in the Bible—an age defined not by the normative but by the imaginative power of J and S. Thus, what we get are reactionary readings of the Bible, such as the treatment of 1 and 2 Samuel in Ryken and Longman, that wash away another kind of "world of experience," that of imagination and sensibility. All the formal resources of "literary craft" are exhibited one by one in the book's chapter on Samuel—plot, wordplay, irony, characterization. Passages from different chapters are presented in succession as illustration. But the sensitive reader cannot help but notice that the chapters associated with S, the Court Historian, pass by just like the others—simply another example of the formal elements of literary composition. Moreover, there is no indication that they stand out from the rest, that they are recognized by most scholars of the historical tradition (that Ryken and Longman claim to so admire) as the product of one of the finest prose writers in the history of literature. And, of course, there is no examination of the sensibility behind the court history.

There appears to be one more chance as we notice that there is an essay toward the end of the book entitled "The Novelist and the Bible." It is written by Chaim Potok, himself a novelist, who traces his emerging experience of the Bible from childhood on. One would expect a story of maturing experience, and this is the story Potok tries to tell. He points to a turning point in seminary school, when he learns from a professor that the Song of Solomon was a "sensuous book" belonging to a tradition of marriage and love songs. And yet something seems terribly missing in Potok's essay. It is the experience of an author reading another author. All we get is Potok reading stories, never the biblical authors. Not once does he try to look for a counterpart in the Bible. He quotes from both books of Samuel but never from S's succession narrative, which some scholars have compared to the modern novel. So what is the purpose for having Potok and the other two writers in the book?

Perhaps they are there to provide contemporary proof of the Bible's literary influence, to which Ryken devotes a chapter, detailing as many influences and biblical allusions as he can. Of course, there is something alluring about getting writers to do the academic work of literary analysis, to talk about the way different devices like figures of speech and imagery are used in the Bible. But how different it is to read Elizabeth Hardwick's small afterword to Jane Austen's *Northanger Abbey*. She begins right away by talking about readers of Jane Austen and making herself one of them. Yes, there is commentary on plot and character, but the focus is on the sensibility of the author and the author's focus on sensibility and culture herself. But where Elizabeth Hardwick knows what she must really confront, Chaim Potok does not. Sadly, neither does anyone else in *A Complete Literary Guide to the Bible*.

11

The Original Student of Origins

Having been immersed in the writings of scholars unable to imagine the culture of David, much less an author, the reader turns hopefully to investigations with such promising titles as *David in History: A Secular Approach* (1986) by the historian of ancient (Greek) history, Jack Cargill. However, with the first sentence, even the most optimistic reader must realize that what is being sought will not be found with Professor Cargill. He begins by announcing himself a "secular historian" who finds the Hebrew Bible "a difficult source to use" because of its suffusion with "theistic explanations of events" and its "highly theologized" narratives. What Cargill intends is "to examine the Biblical narratives without a pro-David or pro-Davidic-dynasty justificatory bias." His focus of study is "David's behavior, what he did, in so far as that can be discovered." He proceeds to deliver what he characterizes as a more "critical" and objective "picture of David," no doubt grounded in history and the historian's skepticism as well as a bit of "educated common sense." As he labors to explain, this is a difficult and painful task because one must sift through the esoteric machinations of biblical scholars, the "desperate literalism" of the theologically possessed, and as well the narratives of the biblical authors, "whose interests are far more theological than historical." Even when he goes to S's narrative for his picture of David, Cargill seems overwhelmed by what he calls a "largely homiletic" narrative. It is ironic that Cargill should become what he most despises and tries so hard to expose.

His picture of David emerges as a literal reading of the books of Samuel and his homily is that of the "secular" academic historian who imagines himself to be more intellectually free and more culturally advanced than the author S. He delivers a one-dimensional portrait of David, believing that it is a critical textual treatment because he gathers in the embarrassing, flawed aspects of David's character from the narrative strands. He believes it to be a secular picture, since he is uncowered by theological taboos. It is all too clear that Cargill has no conception of the culture or the author that produced the succession narrative or, for that matter, the rest of the Hebrew Bible. Moreover, it is evident that he has no interest in offering a picture of that culture or author. There is not even the idea that there should be an interest in doing so. The poor man labors under a blanket of taboos, his eyes all but closed to himself.

The anthropologist Mary Douglas would say that Cargill falters the moment he believes himself to be more modern than the premodern writer of the court history. In Douglas's experience, premoderns can sometimes be more modern than those who study them. We could say that as a scholar of ancient history, Cargill is a student of origins. Yet, he fails to recognize another student of origins—the author S. If he had, he might have found someone less afraid of normative tradition than he is and perhaps more able to confront the origins of history writing and the complexities of culture and sensibility.

About the Author

David Rosenberg is the leading translator of biblical poetry and poetic prose in our time. *The Book of J,* which he coauthored with Harold Bloom, was a national bestseller, and was translated into several languages, from Spanish to Japanese. *A Poet's Bible* won the PEN/Book-of-the-Month Club Prize in 1992, the first major literary recognition awarded to a biblical translator. The former editor-in-chief of the Jewish Publication Society, Rosenberg's poetry and essays have been widely published, appearing in *The Nation, The New Republic, Harper's, Paris Review, Five Fingers Review,* and in the recent cutting-edge anthology, *Primary Trouble,* edited by Schwartz, Donahue, and Foster. Rosenberg has also created a bond between writers today and the Bible's writers in three unique anthologies he has conceived and edited: *Congregation* (1987), *Communion* (1996), and *Genesis: As It Is Written* (1996). **Rhonda Rosenberg** earned her doctorate in interpretive studies. She has written in depth on the subject of civil religion.